Alexandra Psaropoulou

ALL BLOWN UP

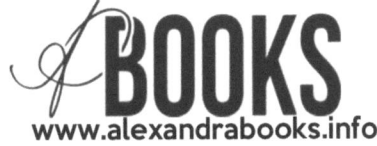

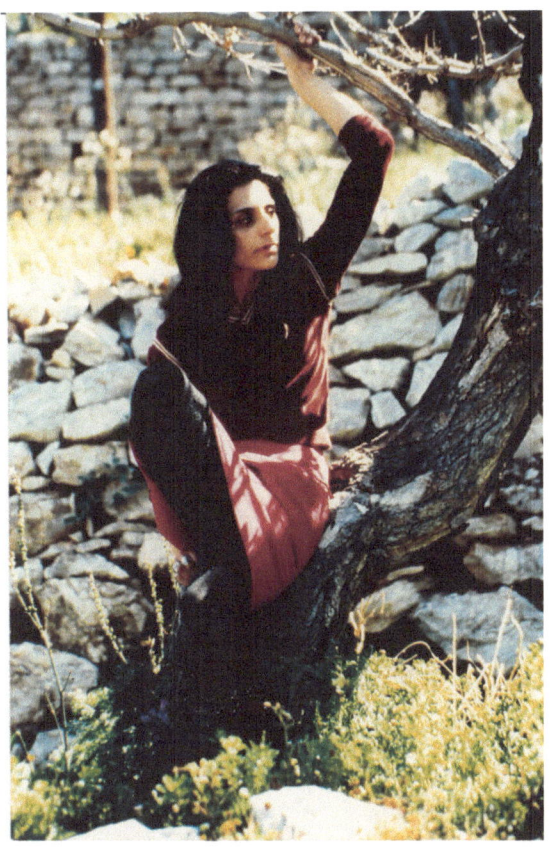

Alexandra Psaropoulou was born on the 12th August 1966 in Athens, Greece in the year of the horse of fire. At the age of 16, she went to England to continue her studies at St.Mary's in Wiltshire and Anglia Ruskin in Cambridge. She lived in Paris for a year and New York for a year, before returning to Greece to settle. Her father was a renowned poet and author and had a successful publishing company in Greece. Her mother was a ballet dancer, critic, and teacher as well as president of the Dance Union in Greece. Her family social circles, ever since a little girl, were rich with artists, writers, and academics. She lives with her husband, a classical guitar soloist, and four children outside of Athens by the sea and publishes her own poetry on Amazon. Each of Alexandra's books is a symphony composed of a long poem accompanied by graphic illustrations that convey "The Flying".

Copyright©
Alexandra Psaropoulou

The right of Alexandra Psaropoulou to be identified as author of this work has been asserted by her accordance with section 77 and 78 of the Copyright, Designs and Patents Act 1988.

All rights reserved. No part of this publication may be reproduced, stored in a retrieval system, or transmitted in any form or by any means, electronic, mechanical, photocopying, recording, or otherwise, without her permission.

Any person who commits any unauthorized act in relation to this publication may be liable to criminal prosecution and civil claims for damages.

New edition 2020
AlexandraBooks.info
San Francisco, California

To my family for all their support.

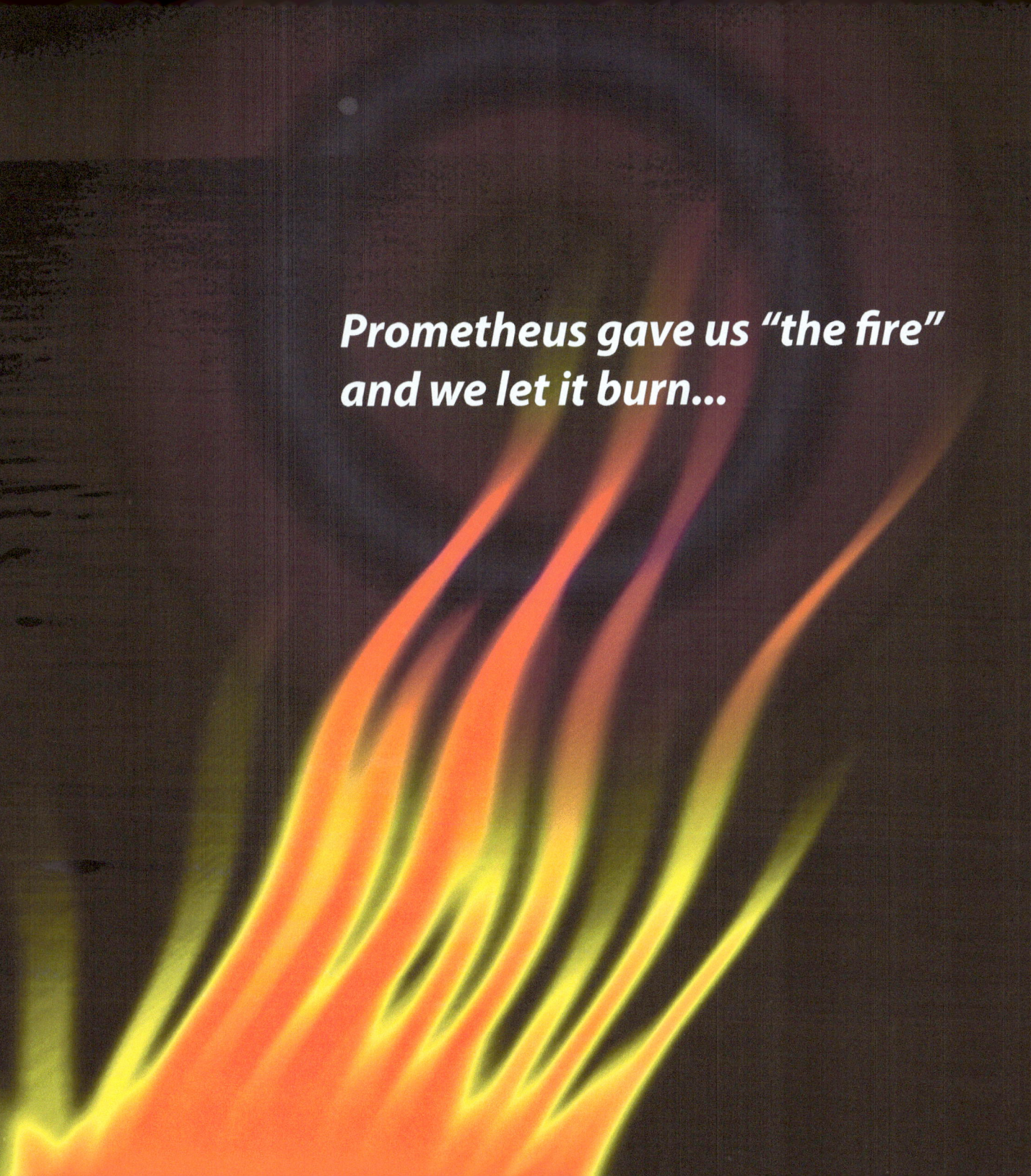

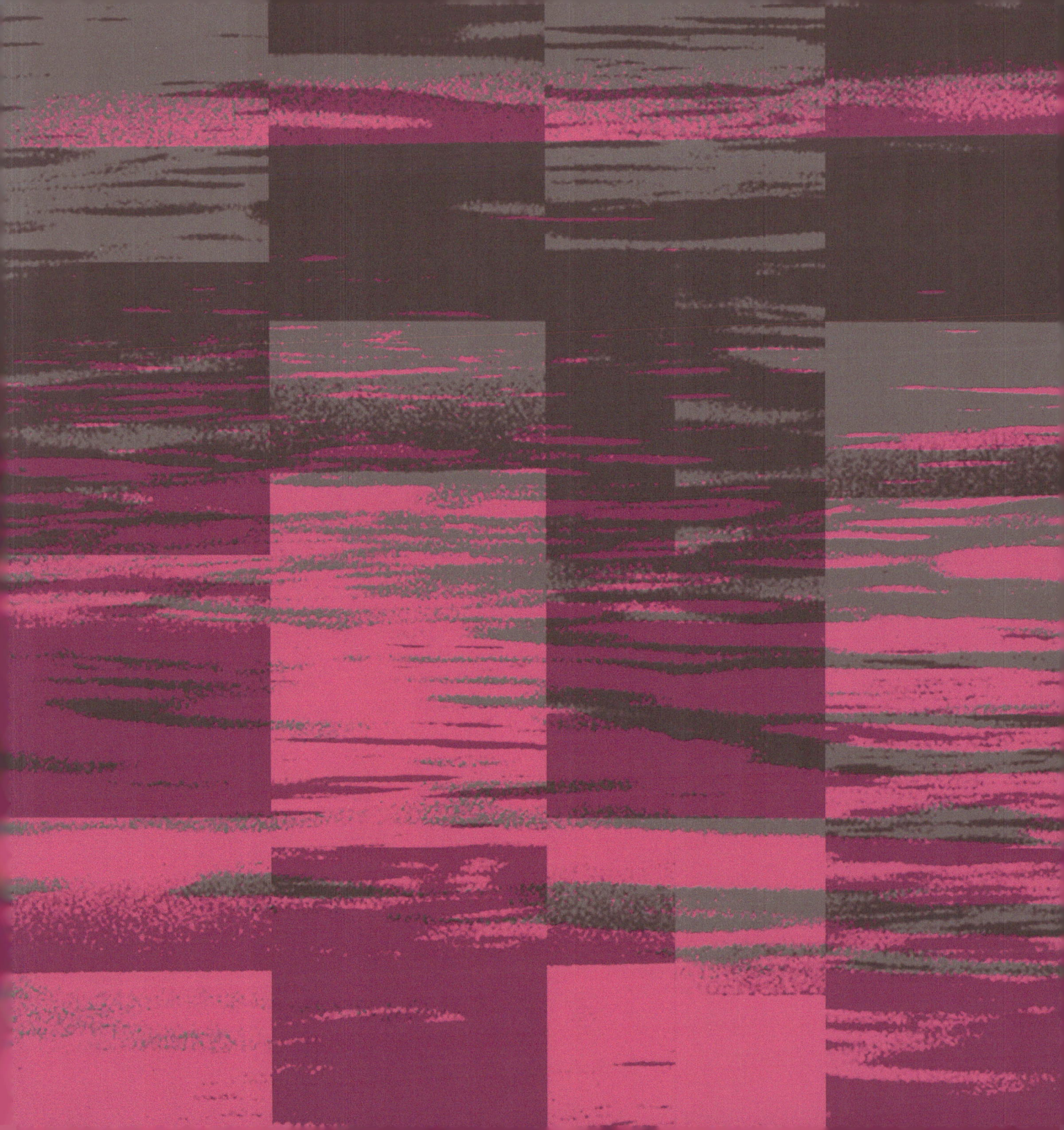

I'll keep on running
even if my visions go wild

and I bravely follow them

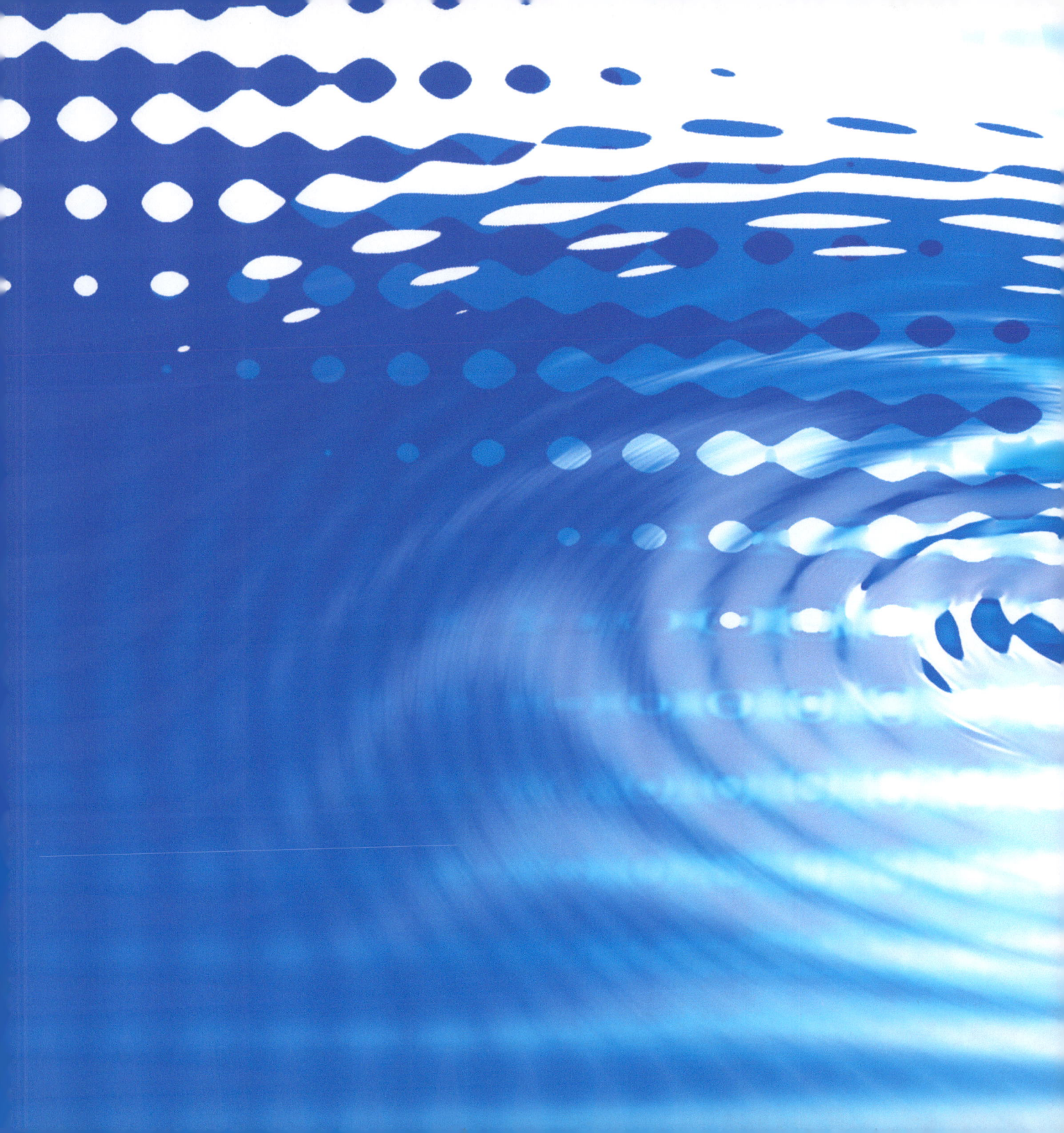

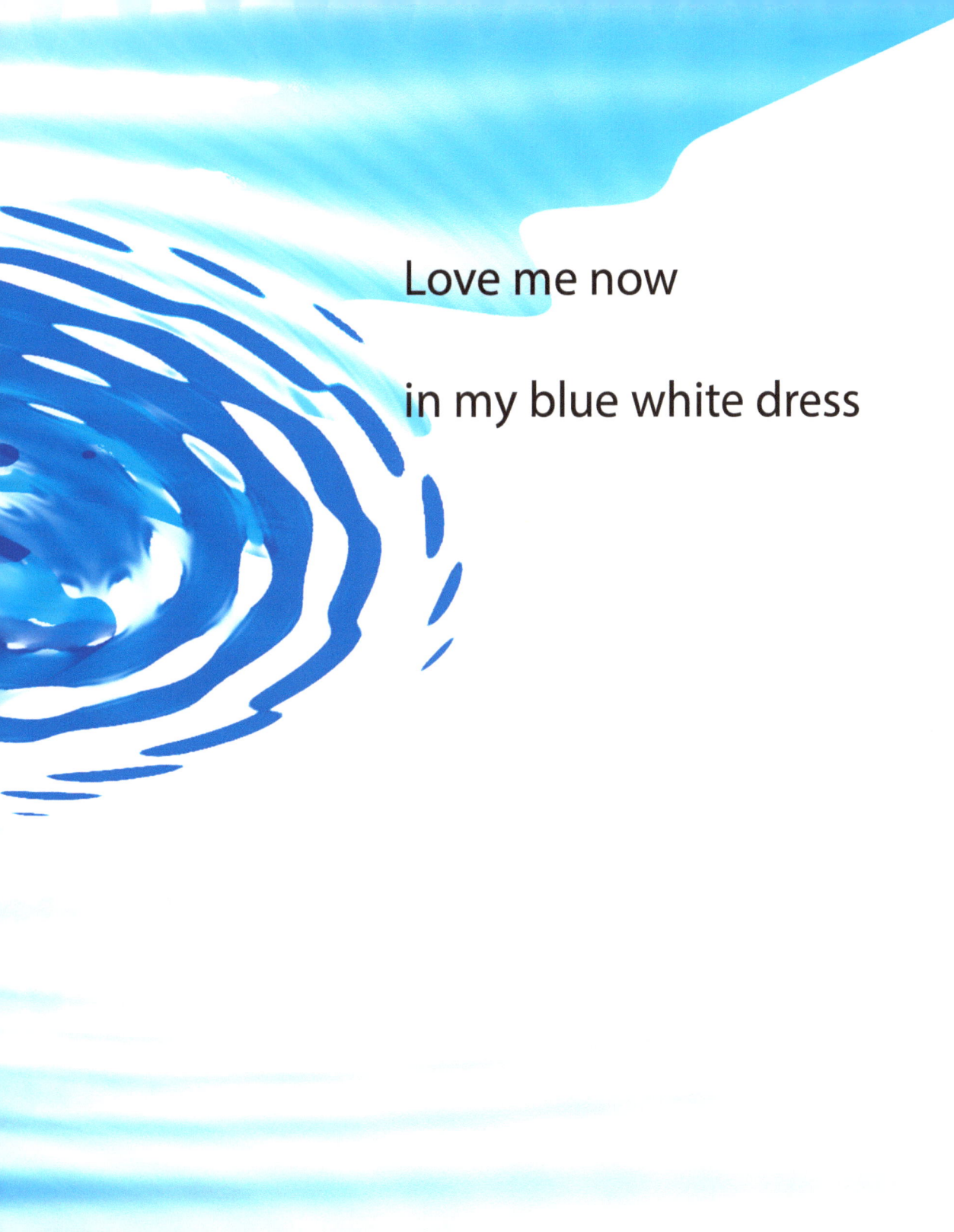

Love me now

in my blue white dress

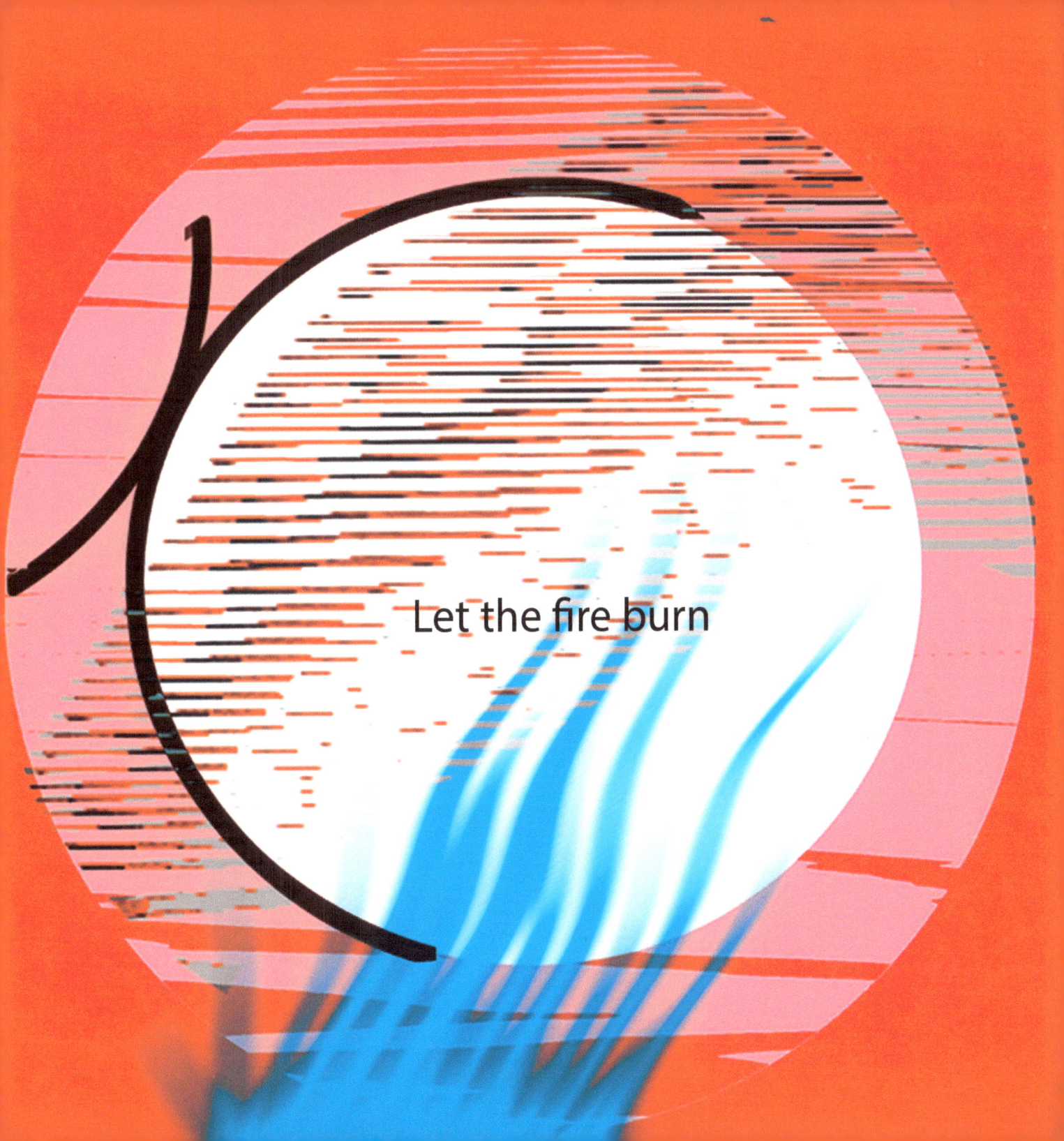

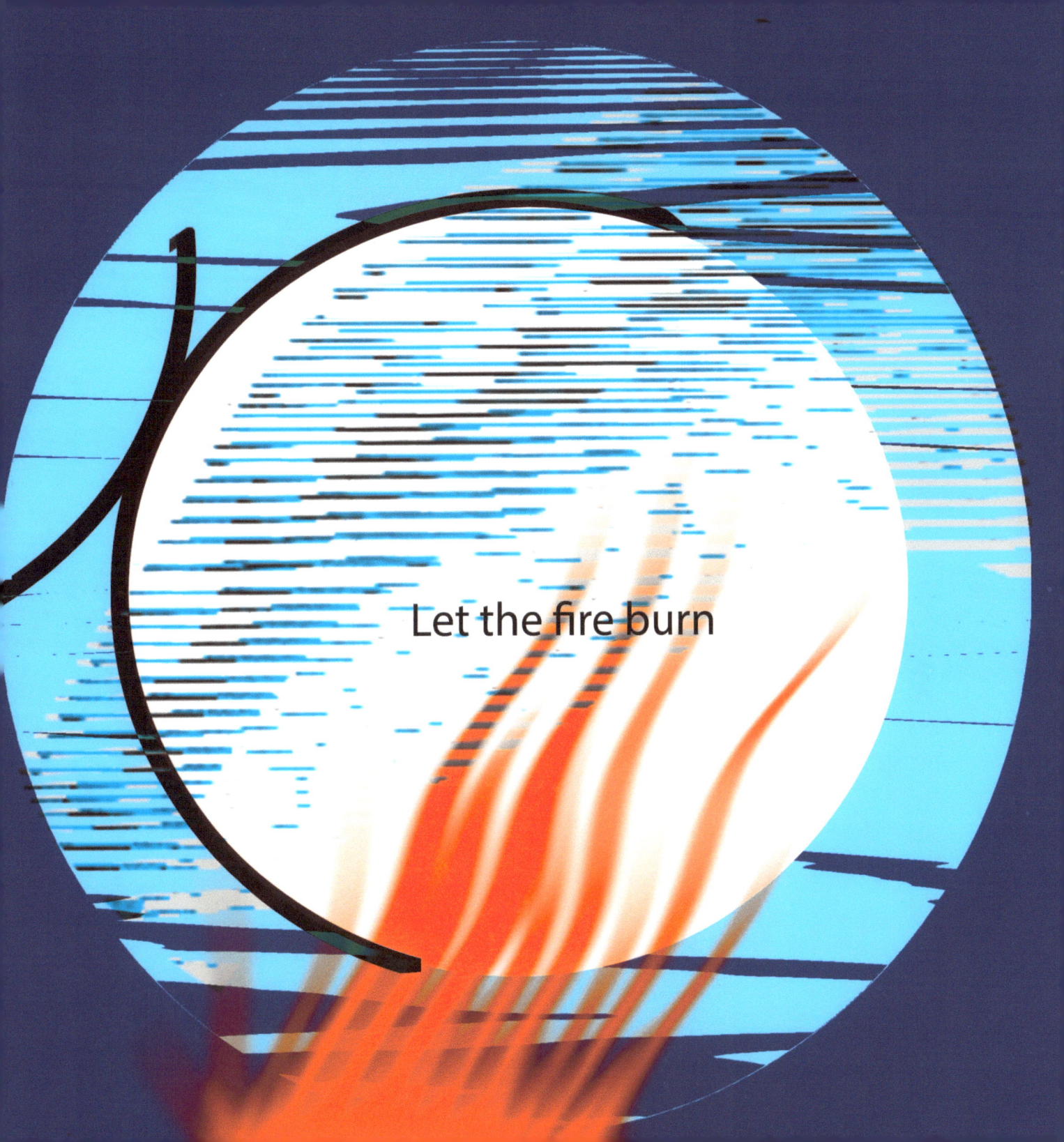

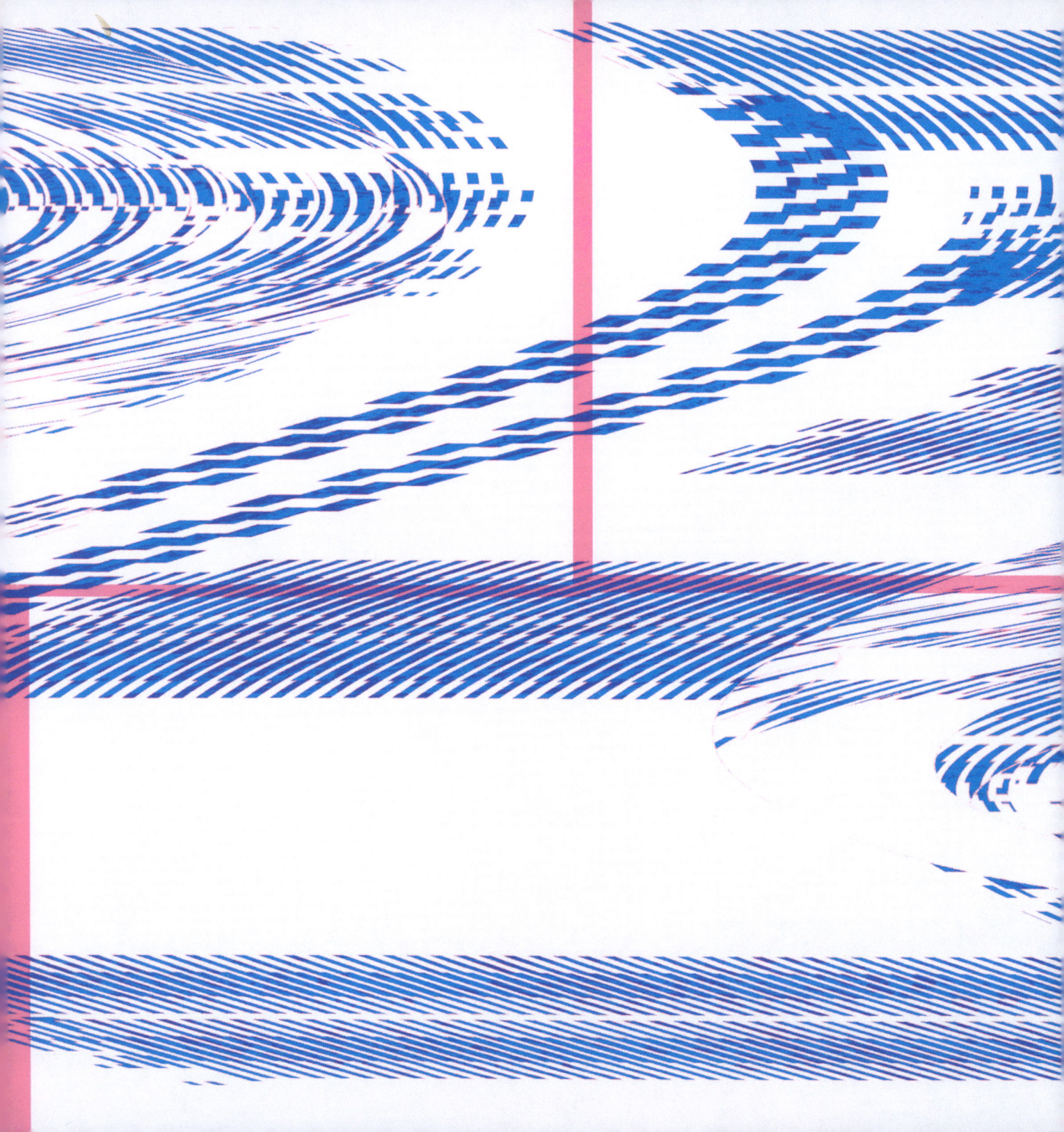

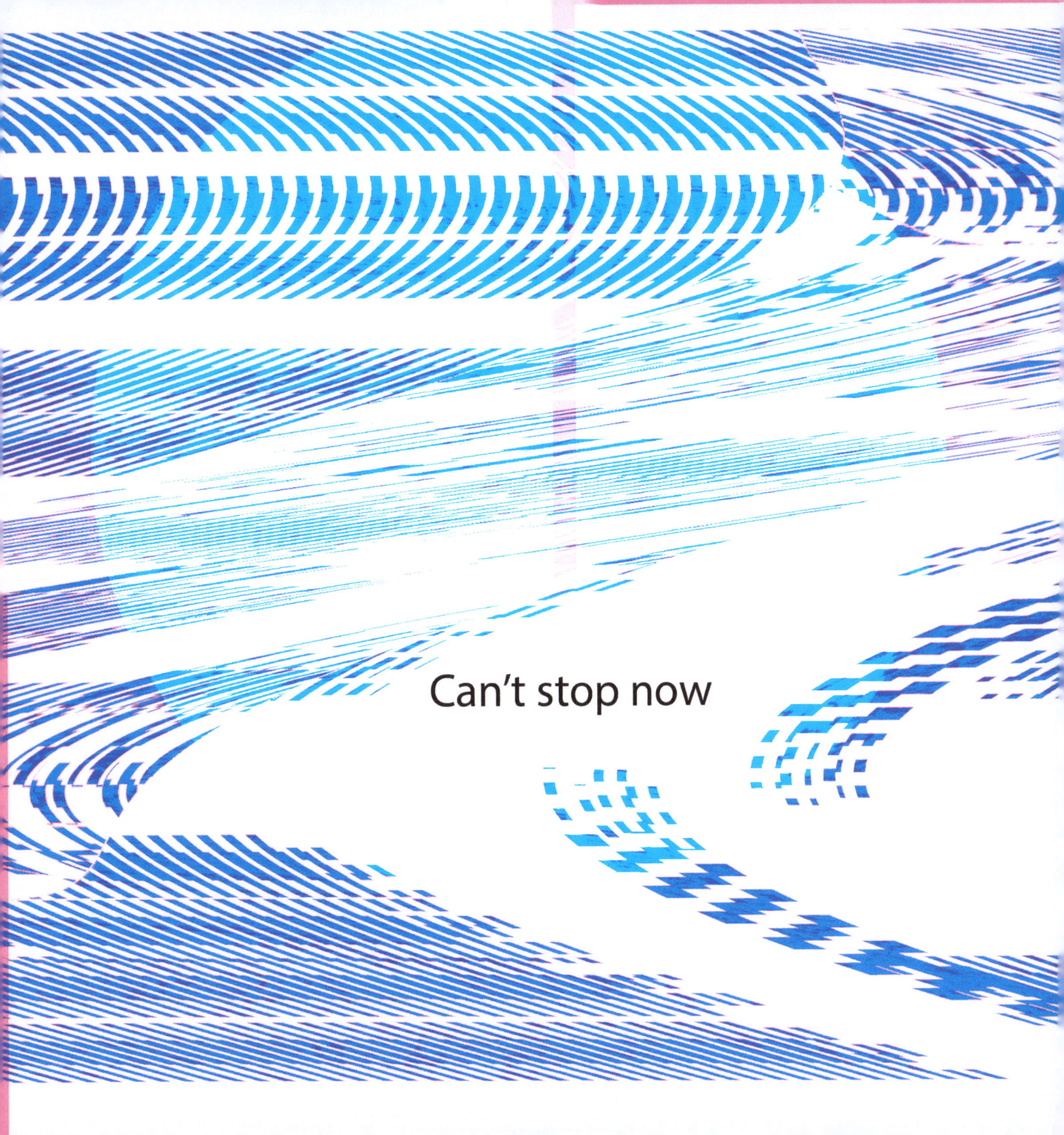

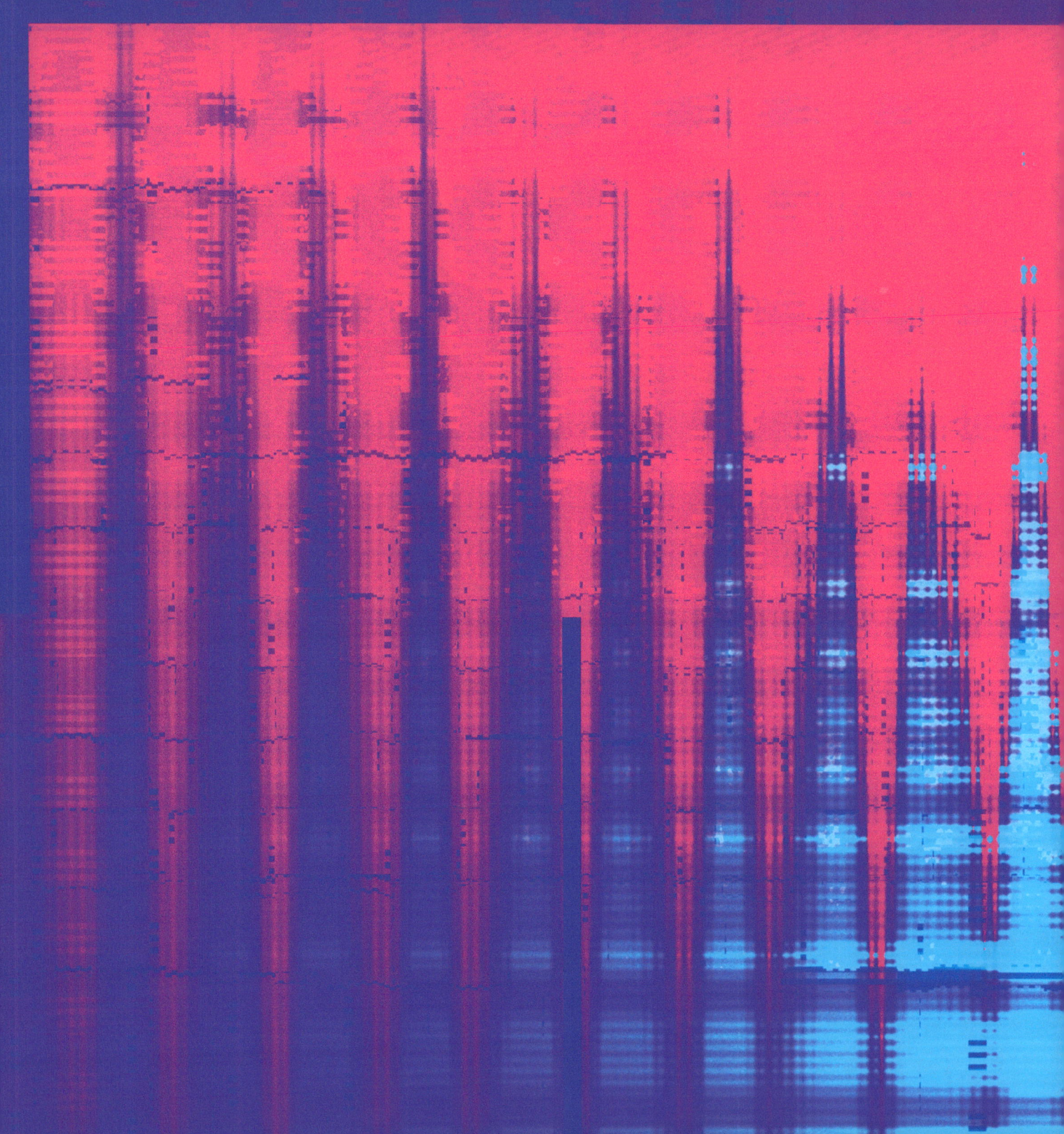

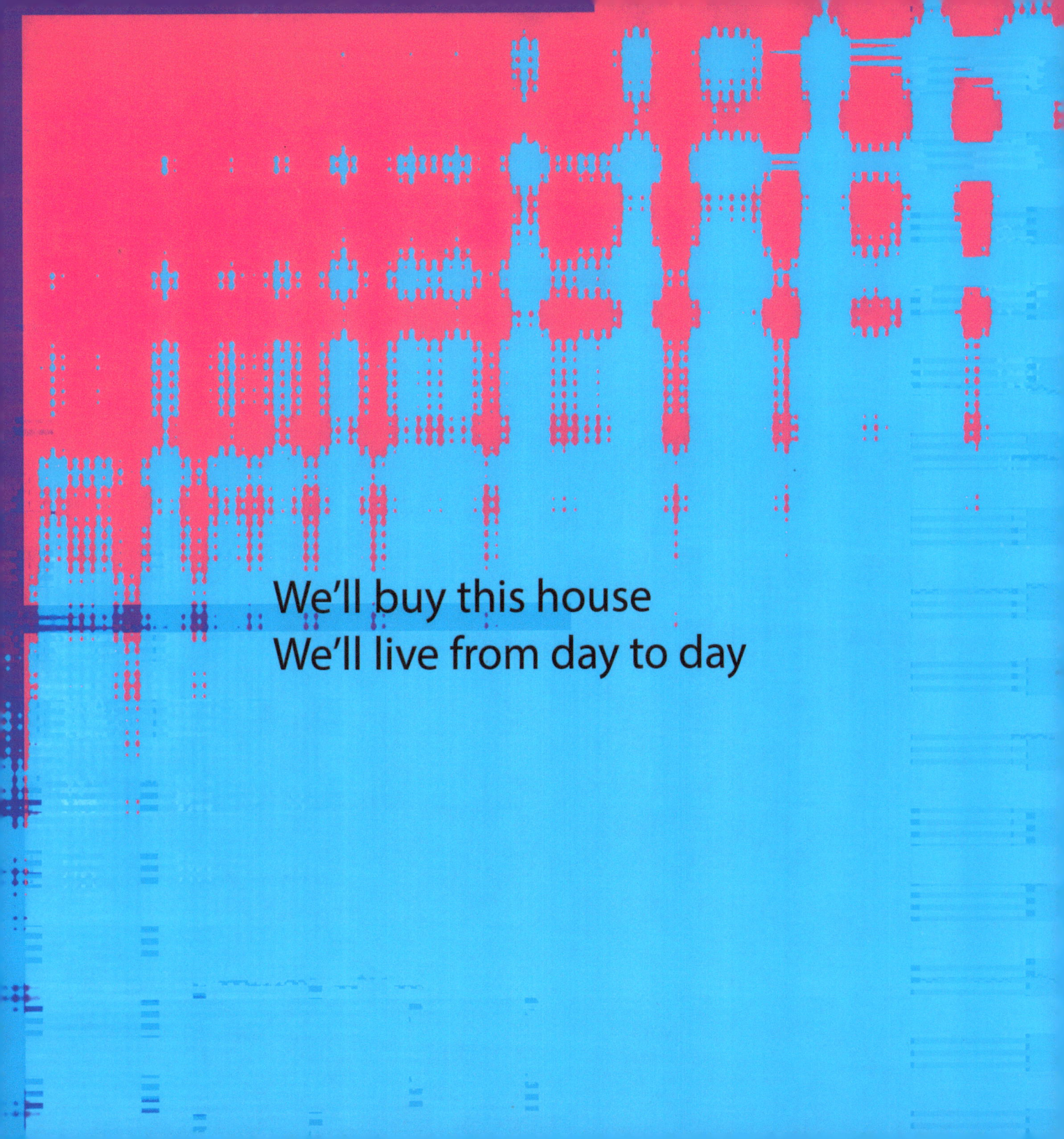

Get me out
before it's all over

Take me out
make it so good
before I'm all torn up

under the starlit sky

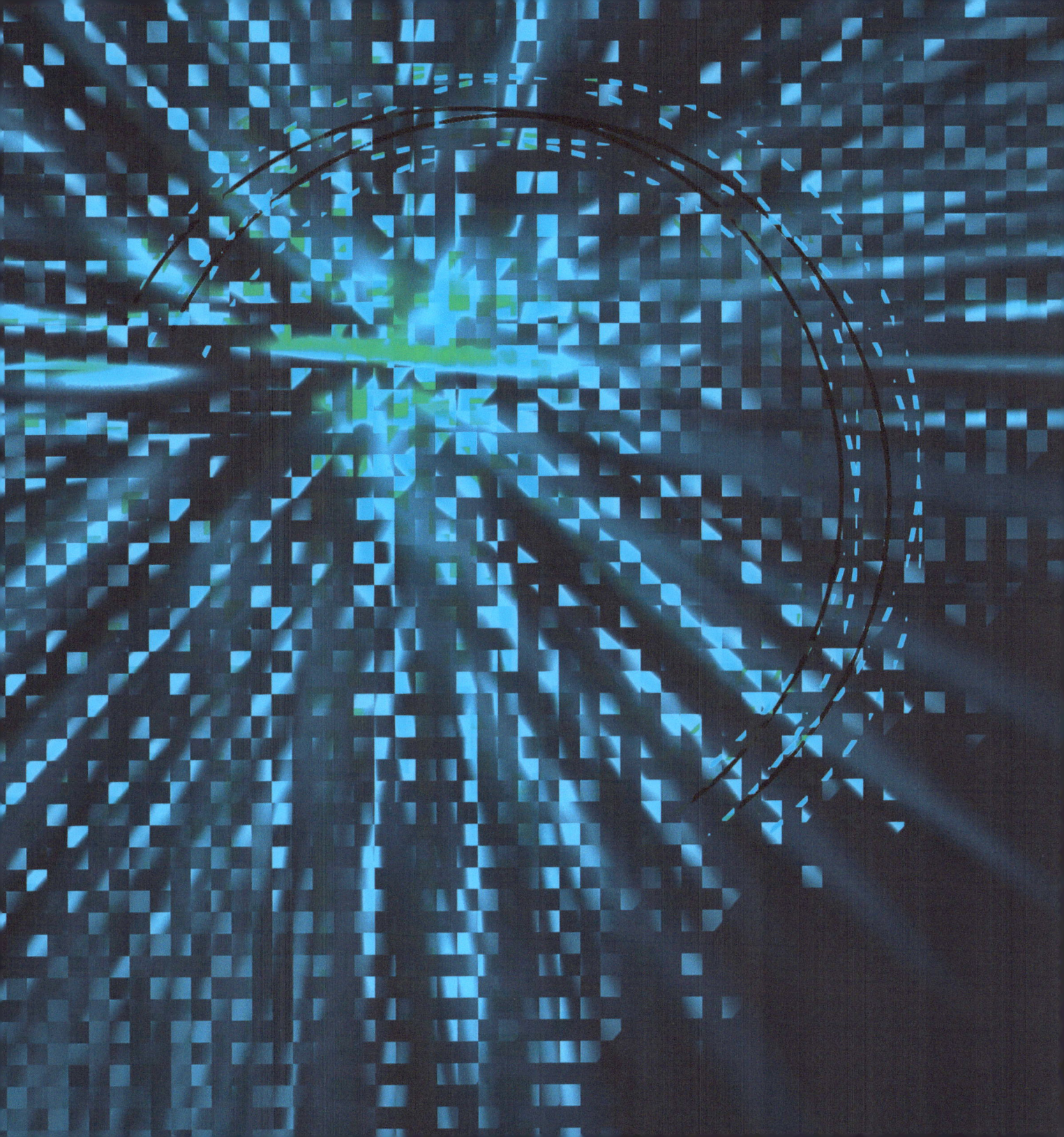

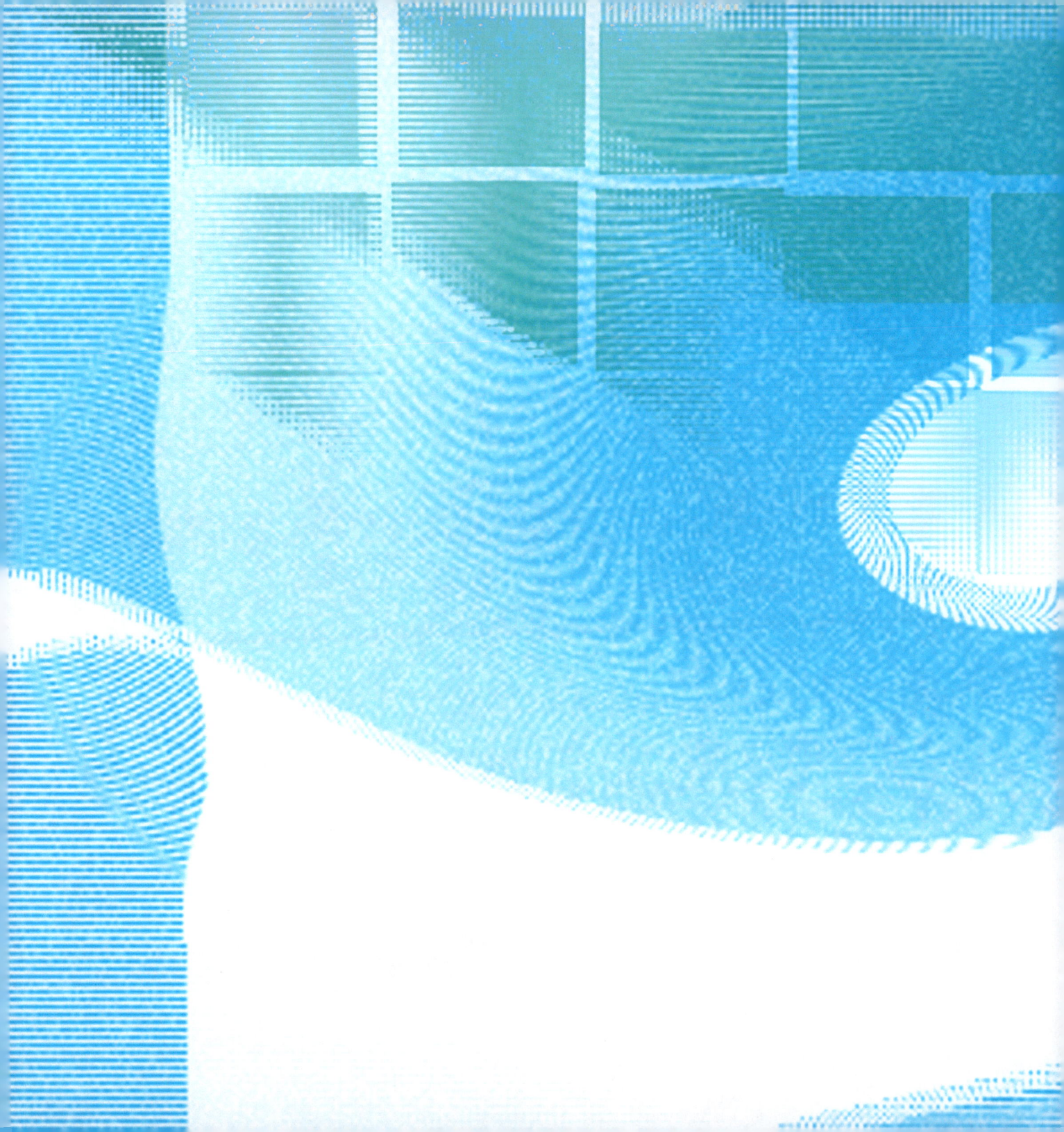

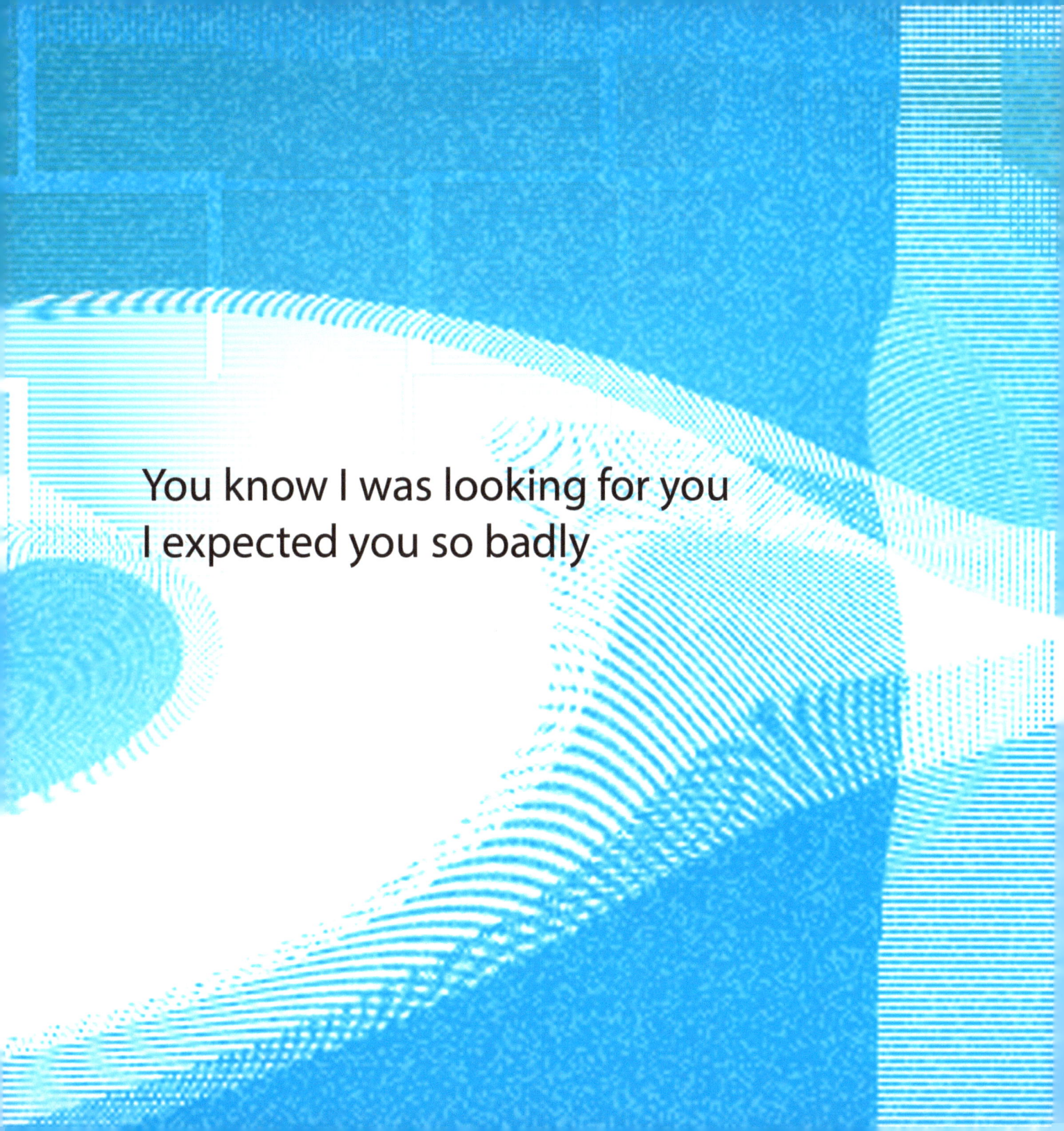

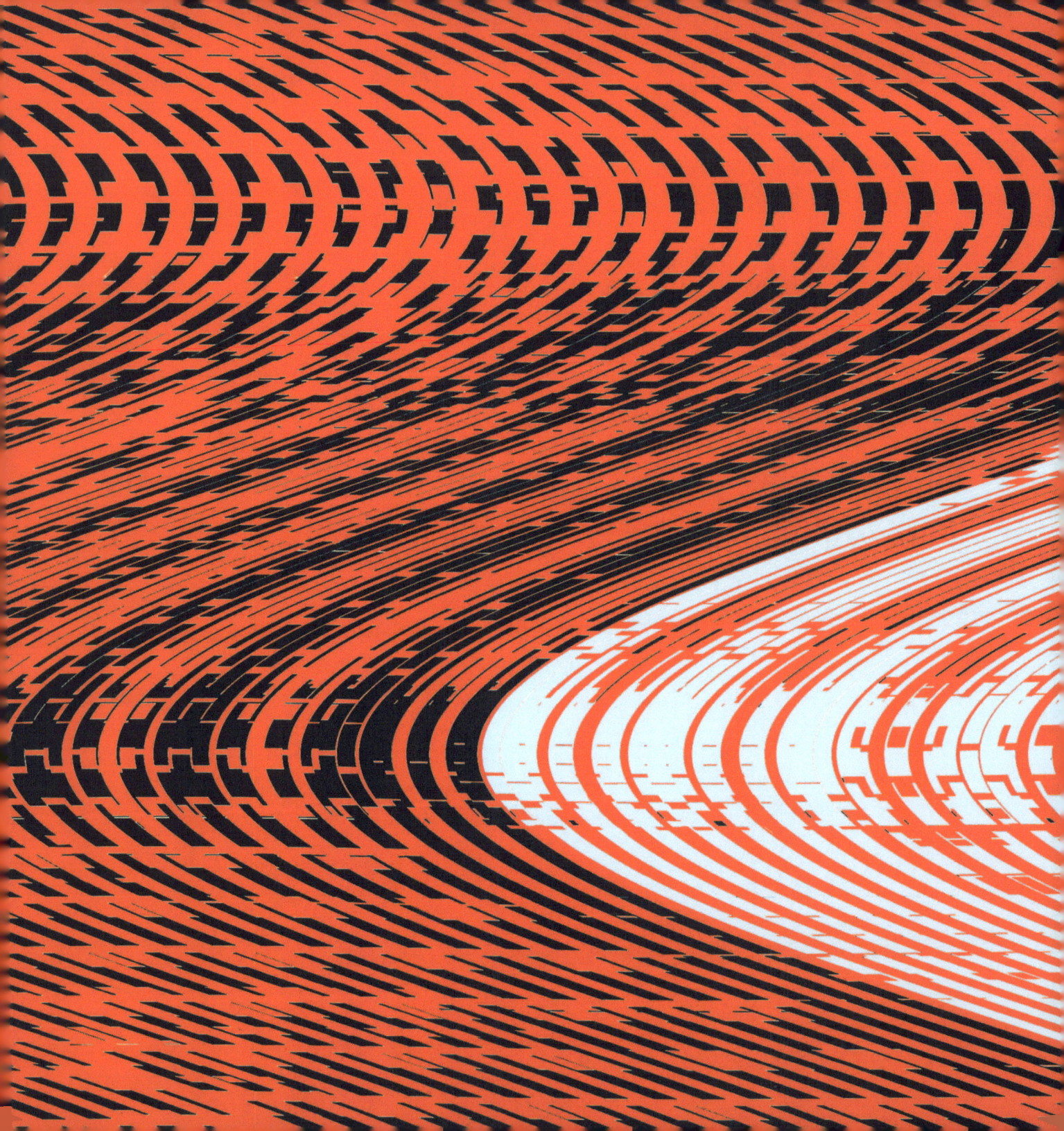

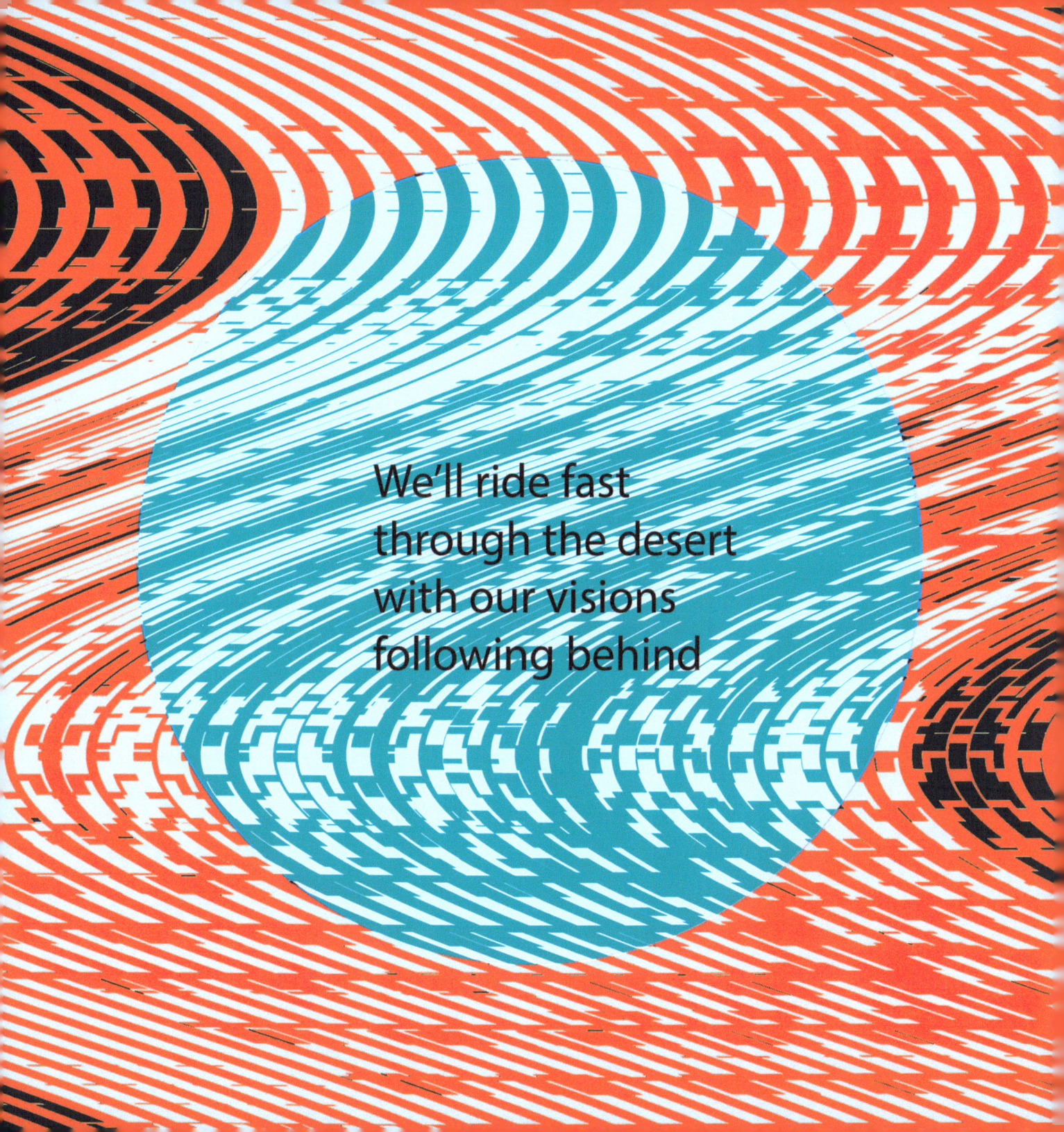

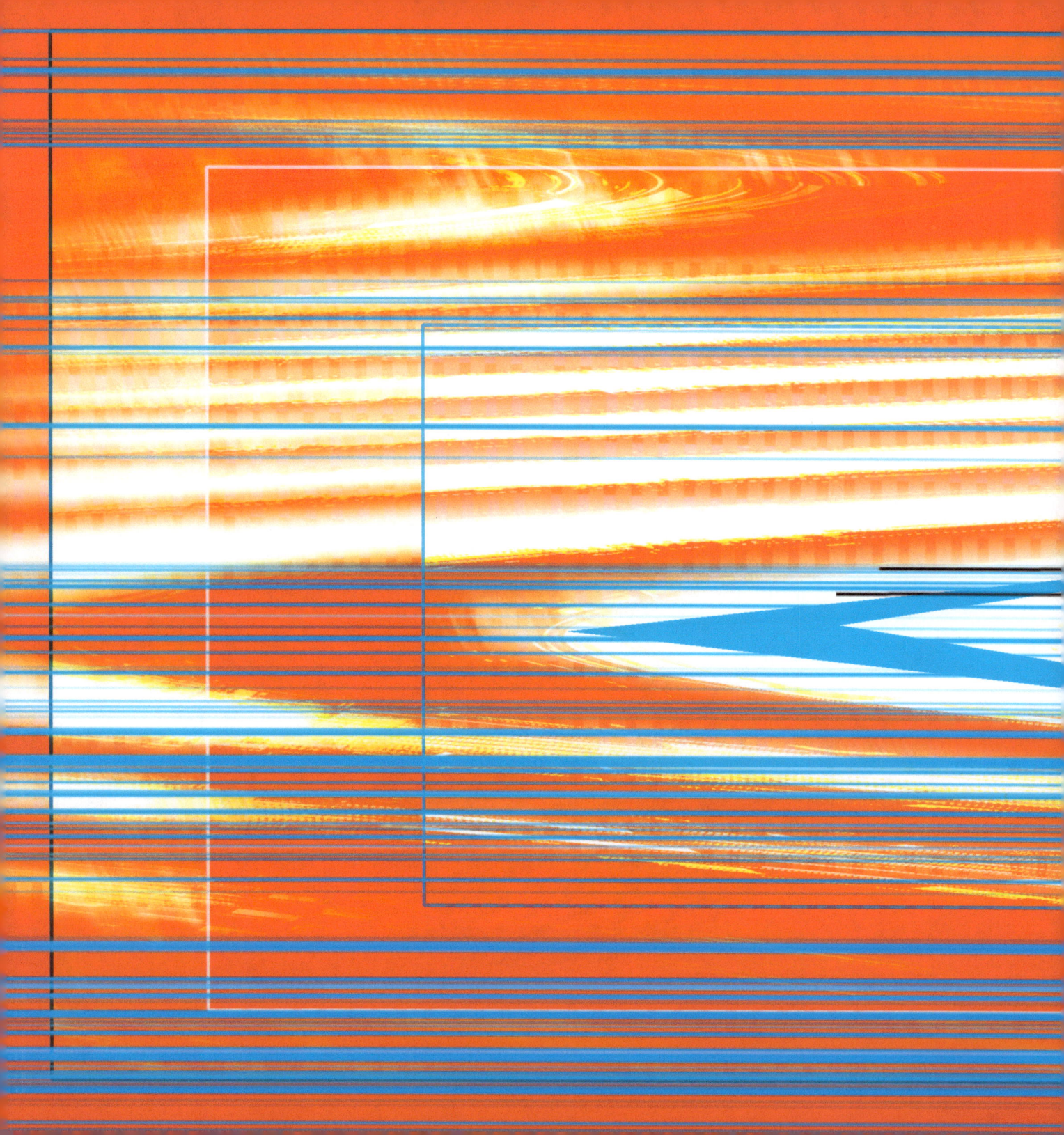

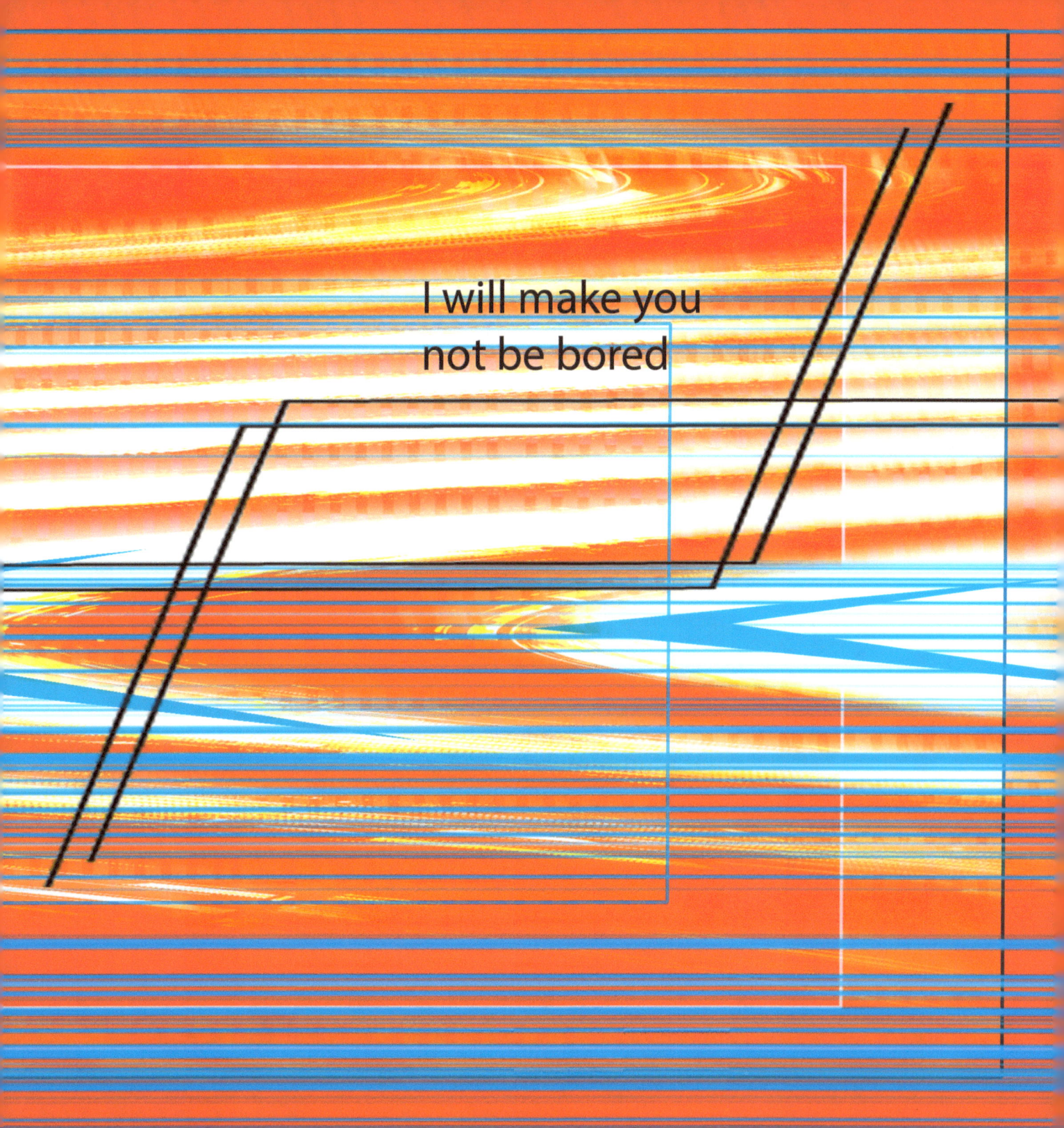

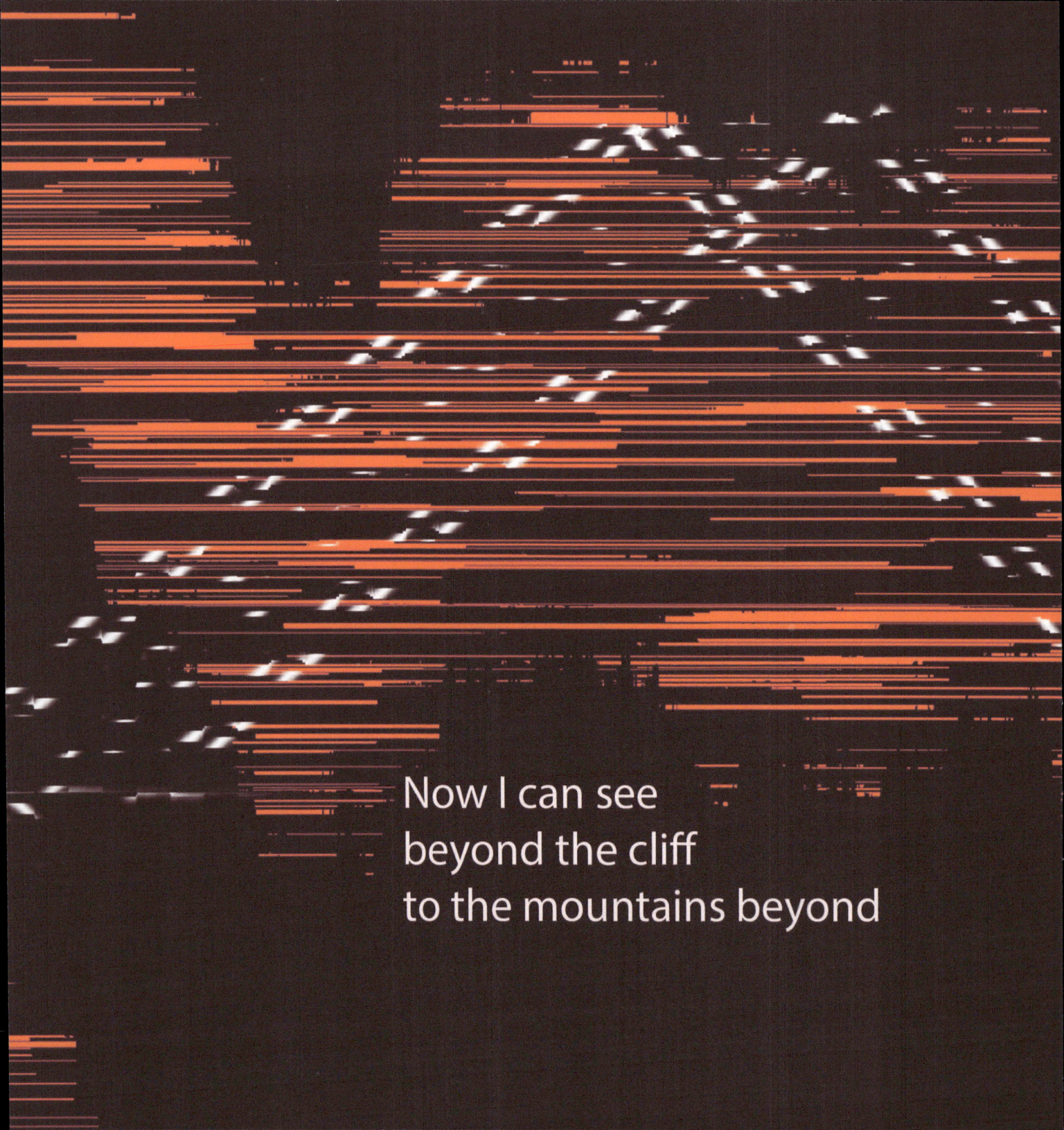

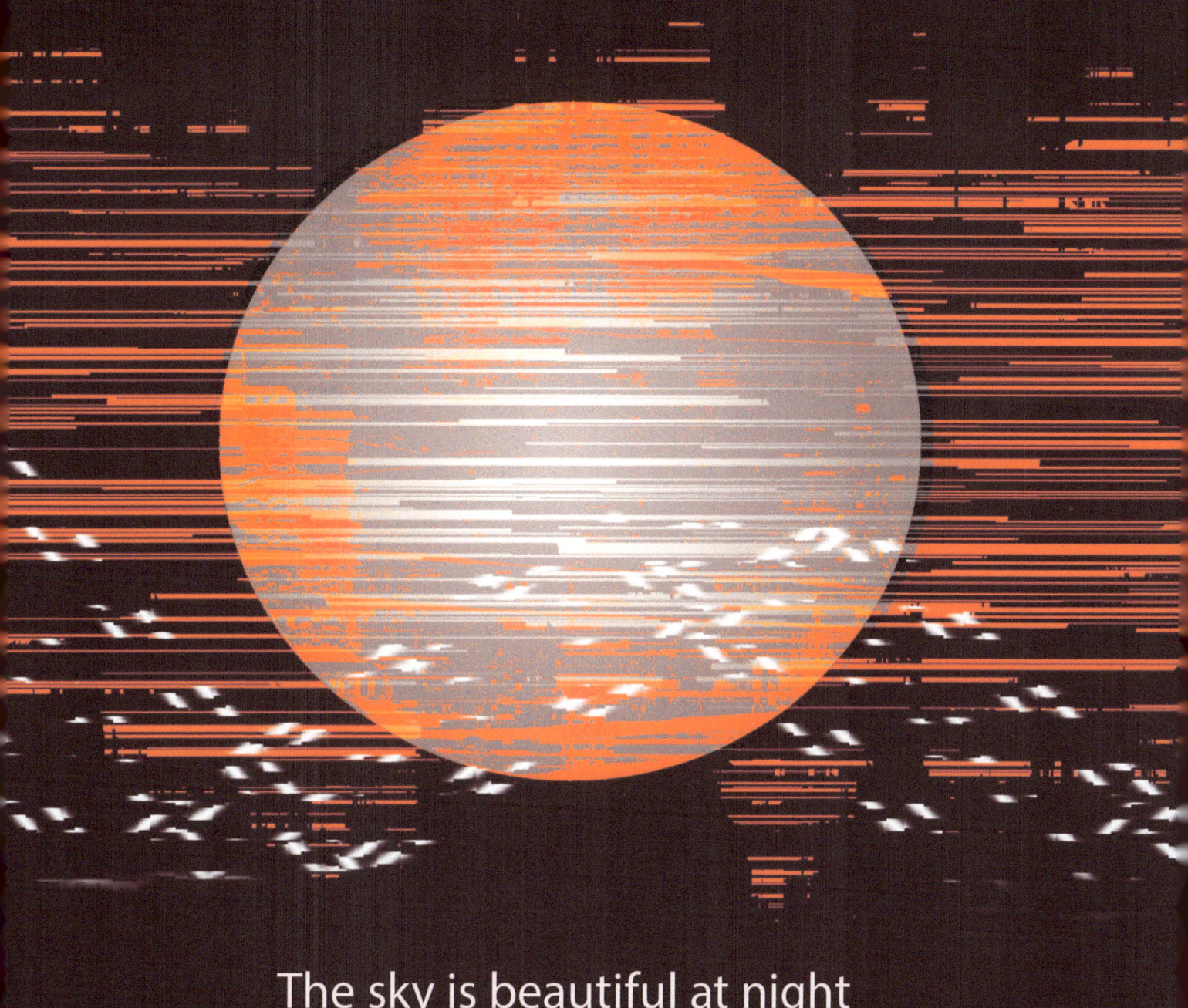

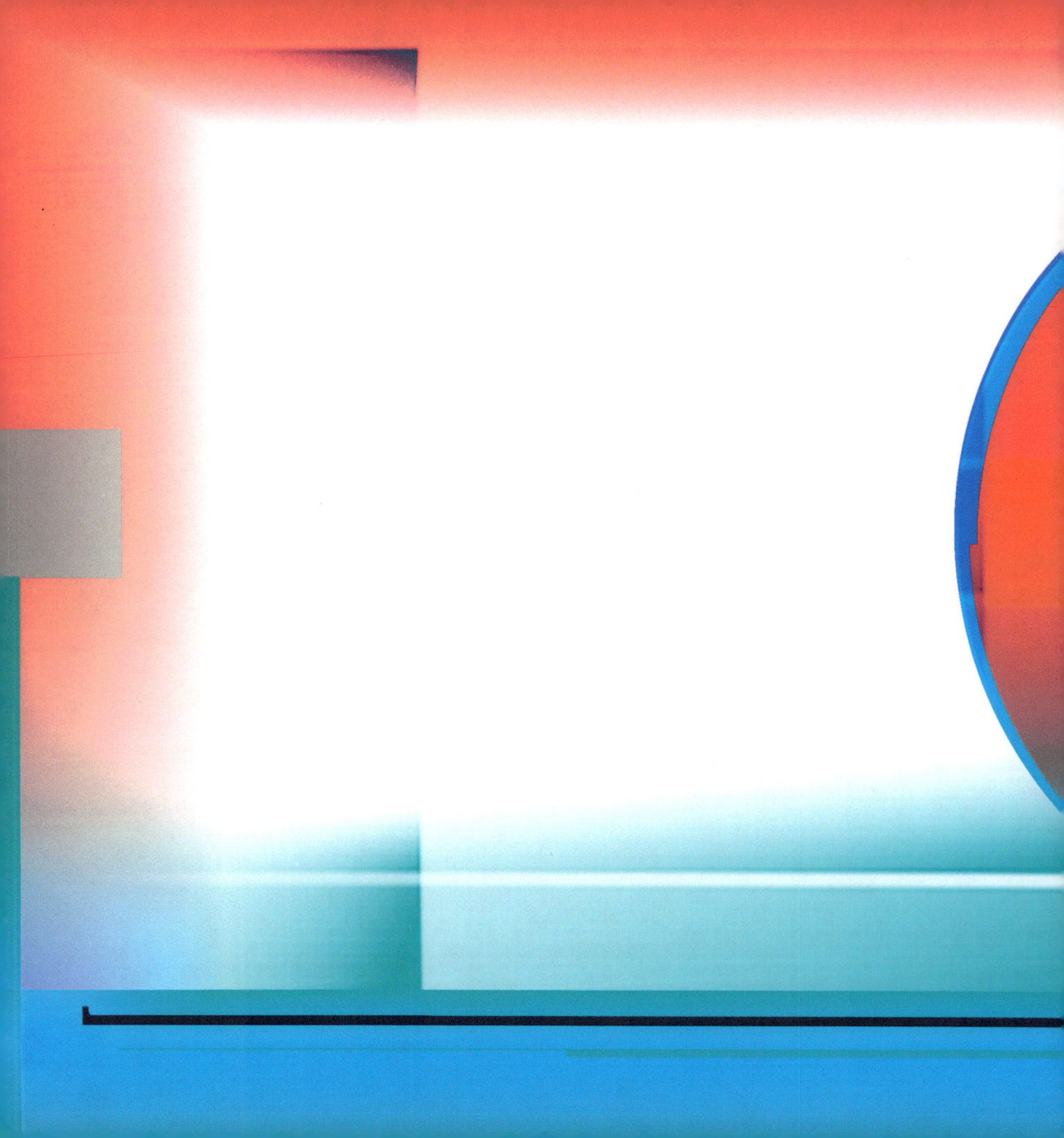

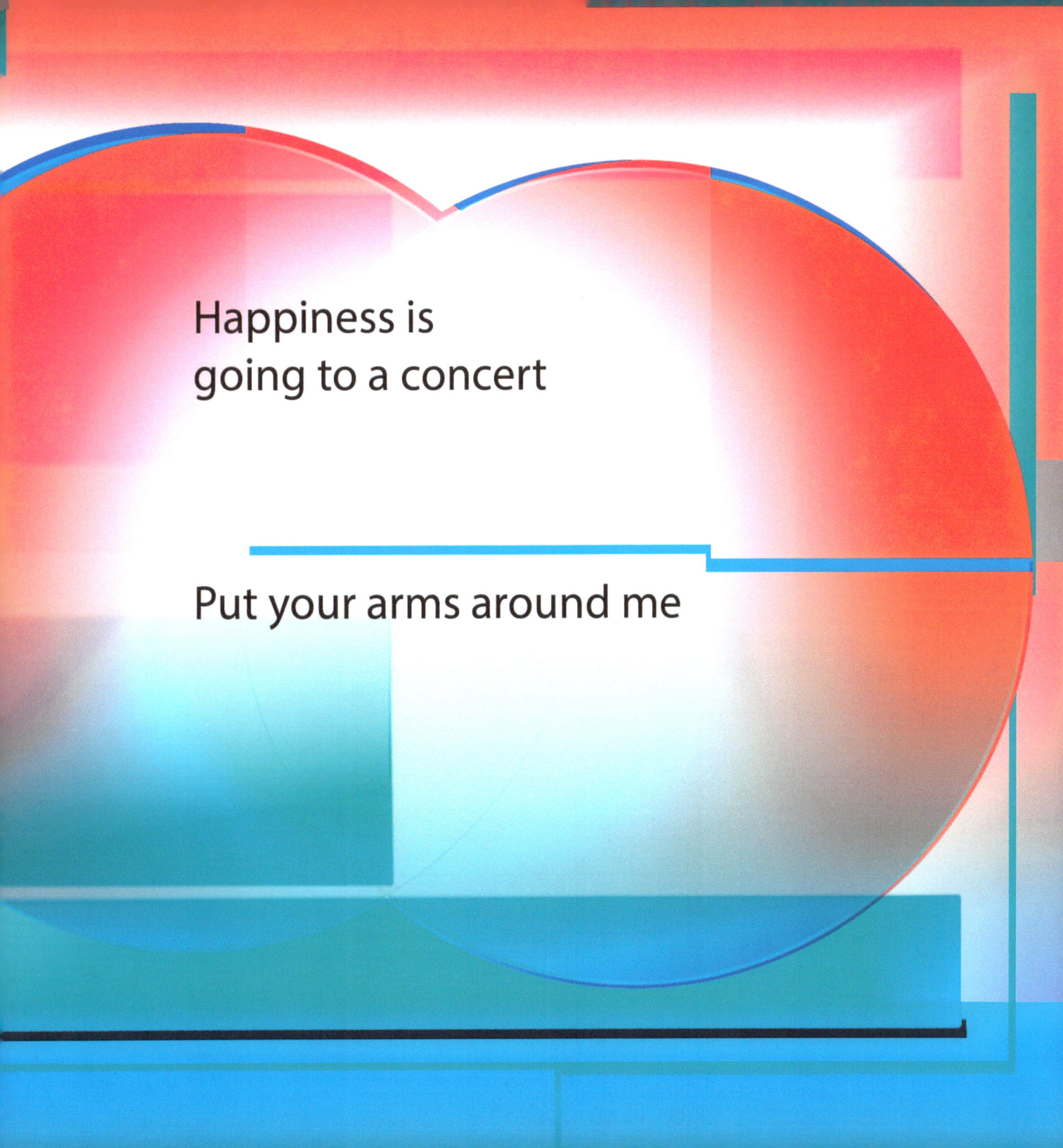

Happiness is
going to a concert

Put your arms around me

Make me cry/laugh

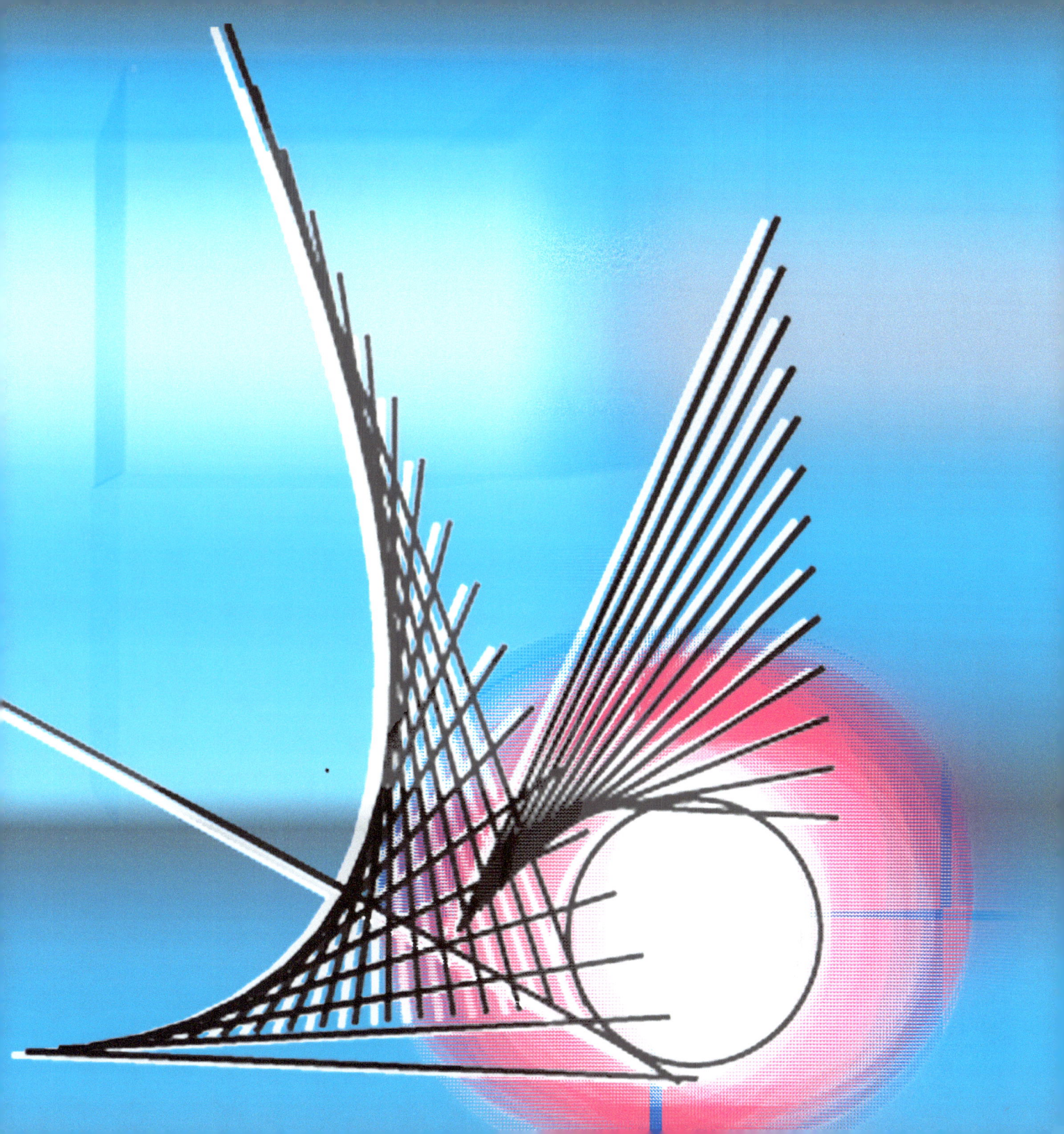

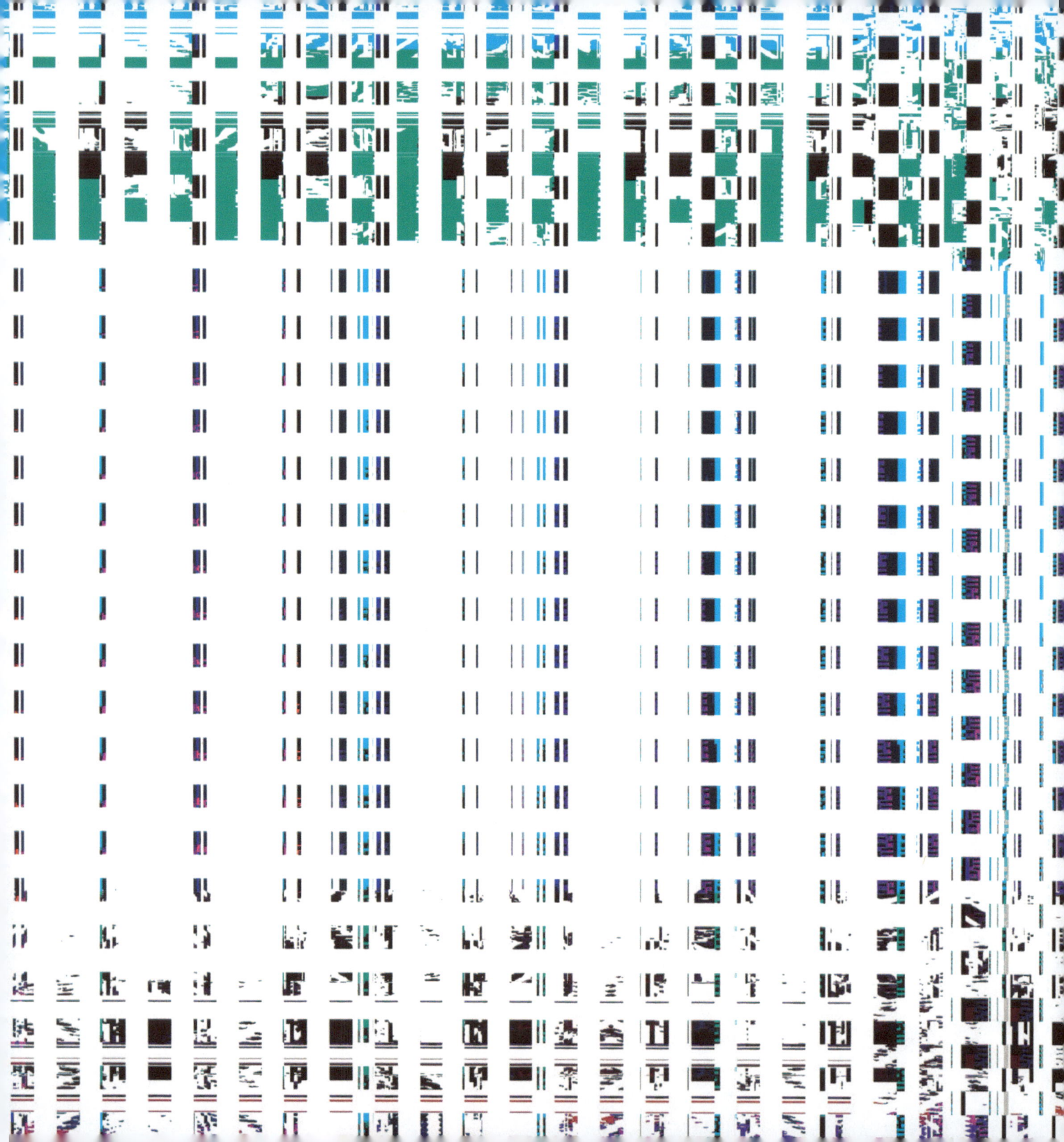

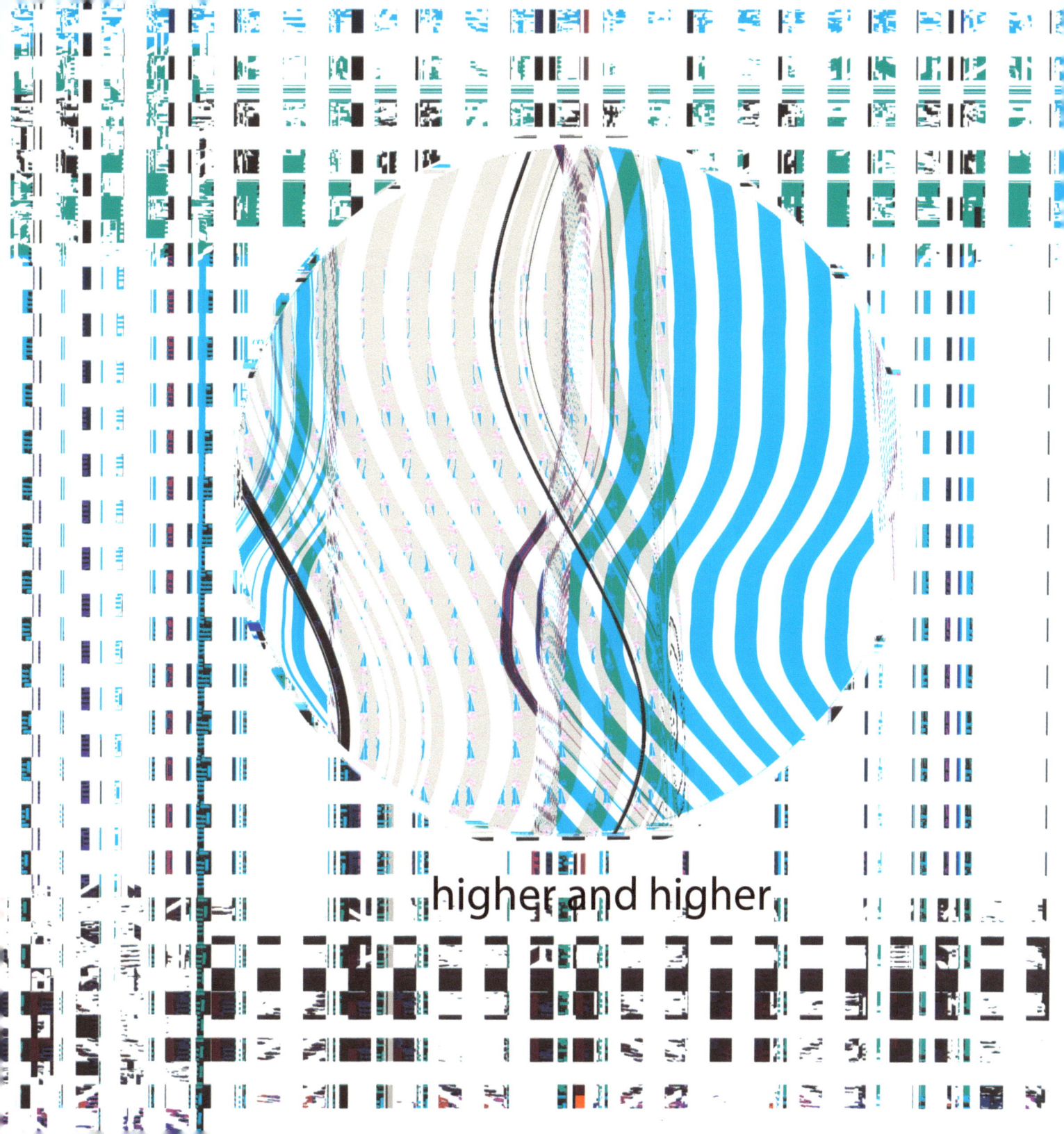

I love you

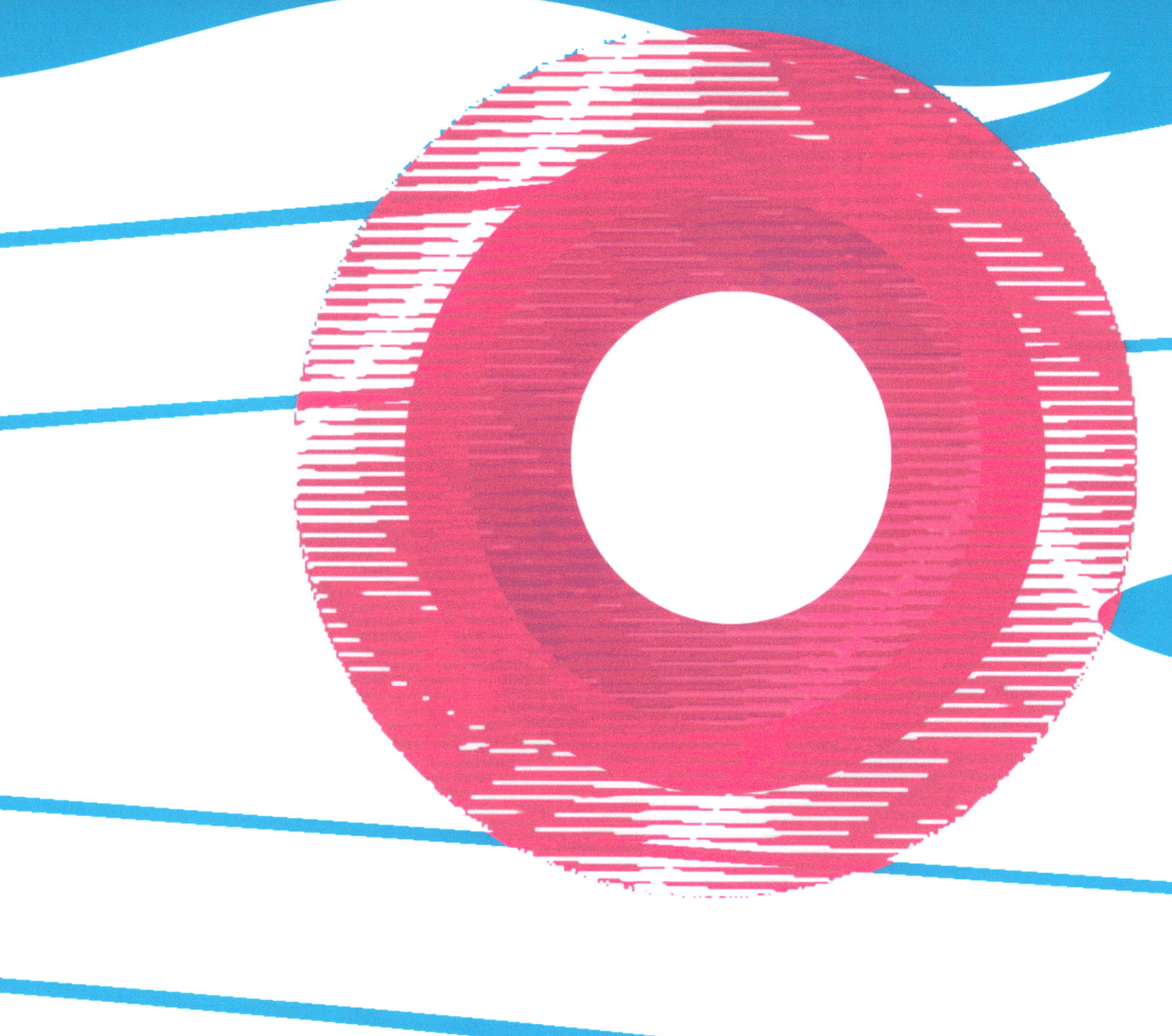

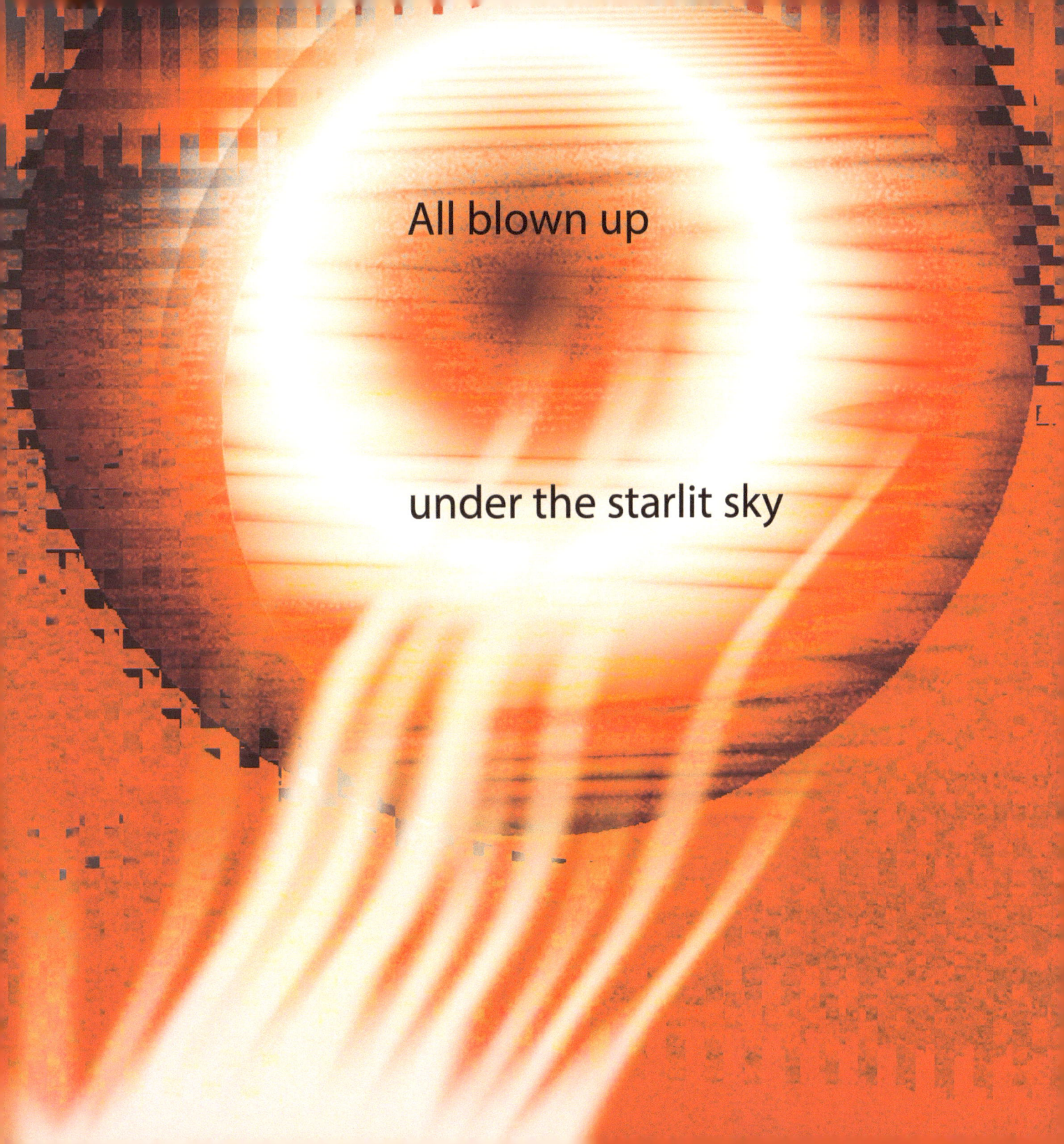

The rain
will be coming down

There'll be millions of people
all around

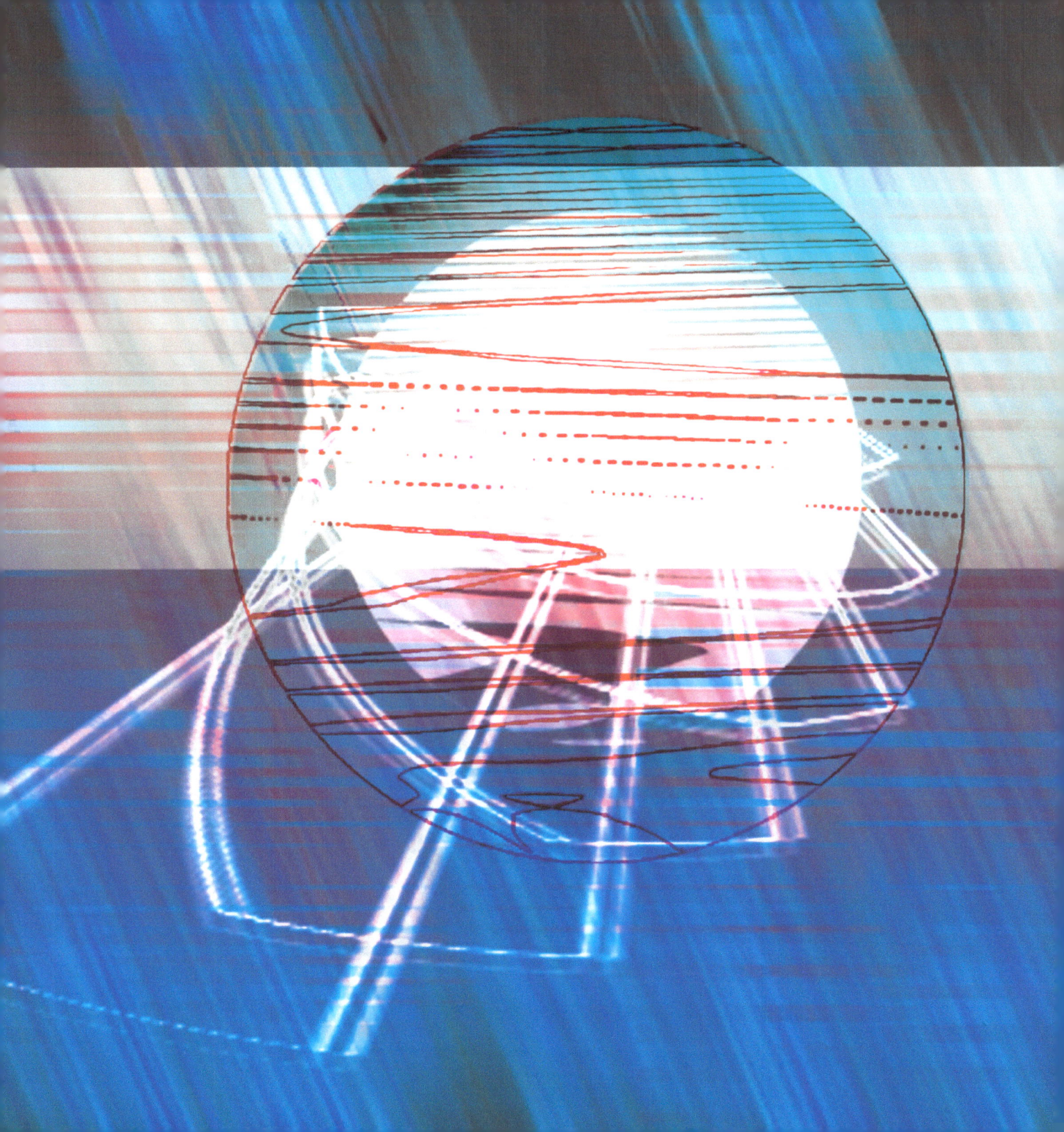

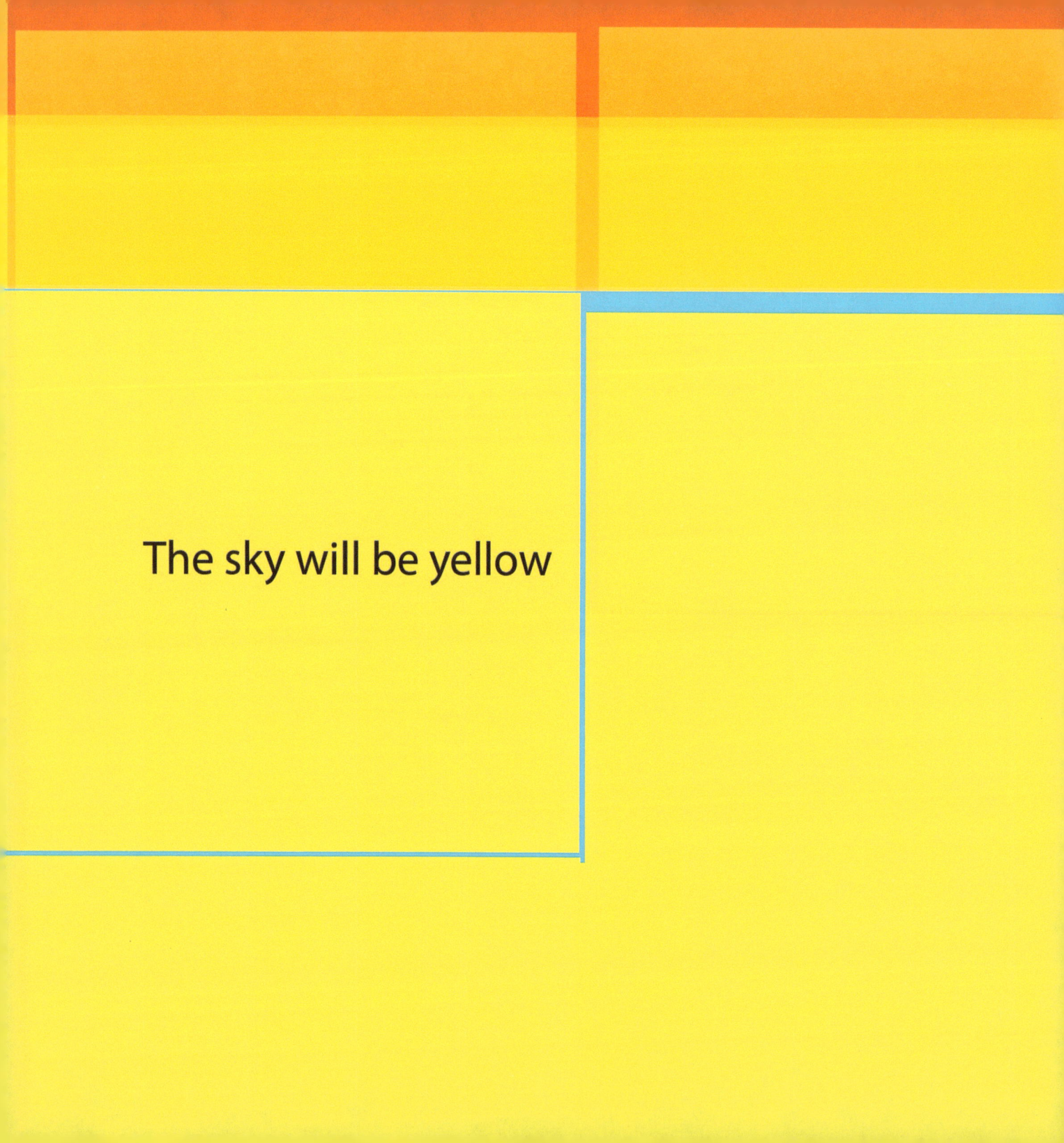

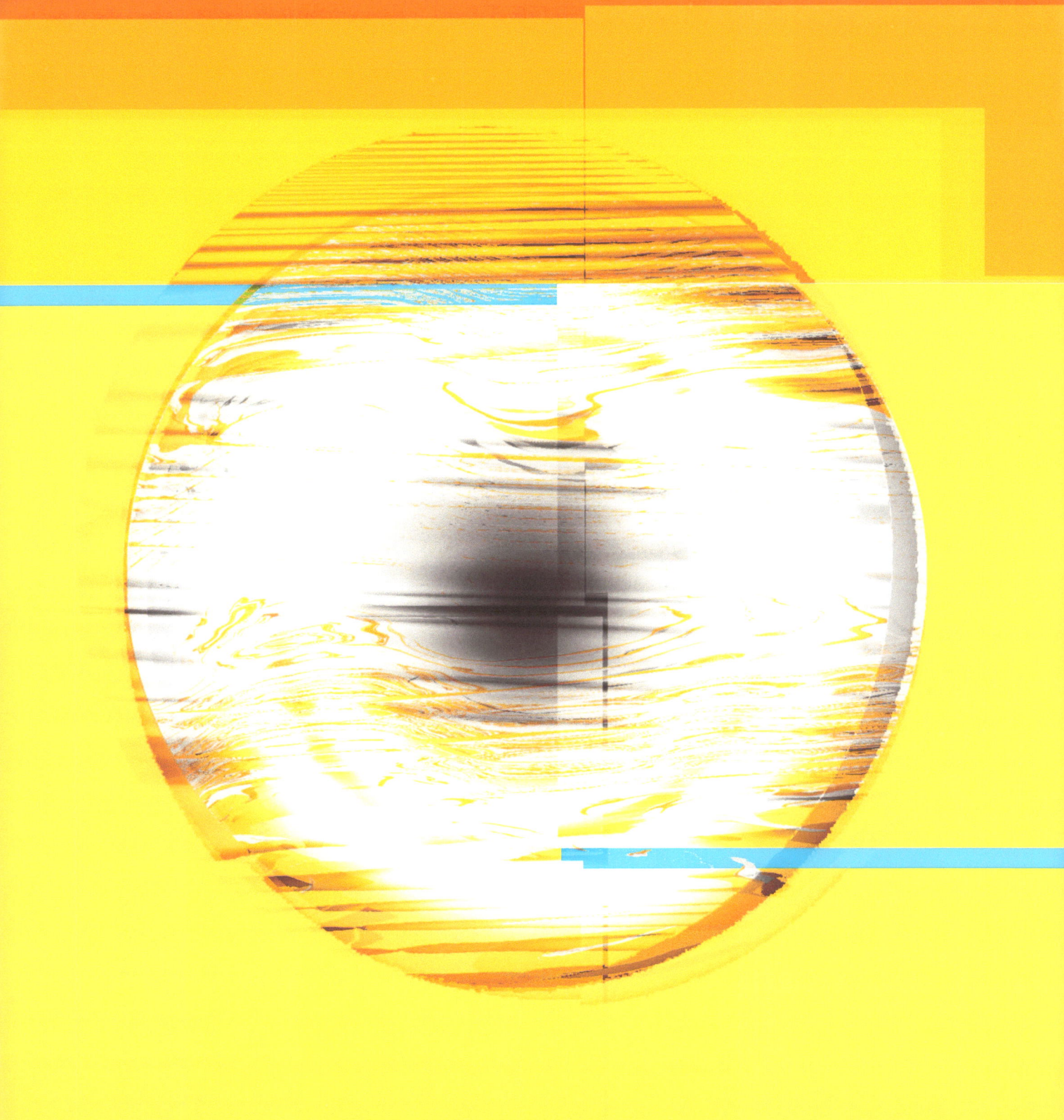

till it happens

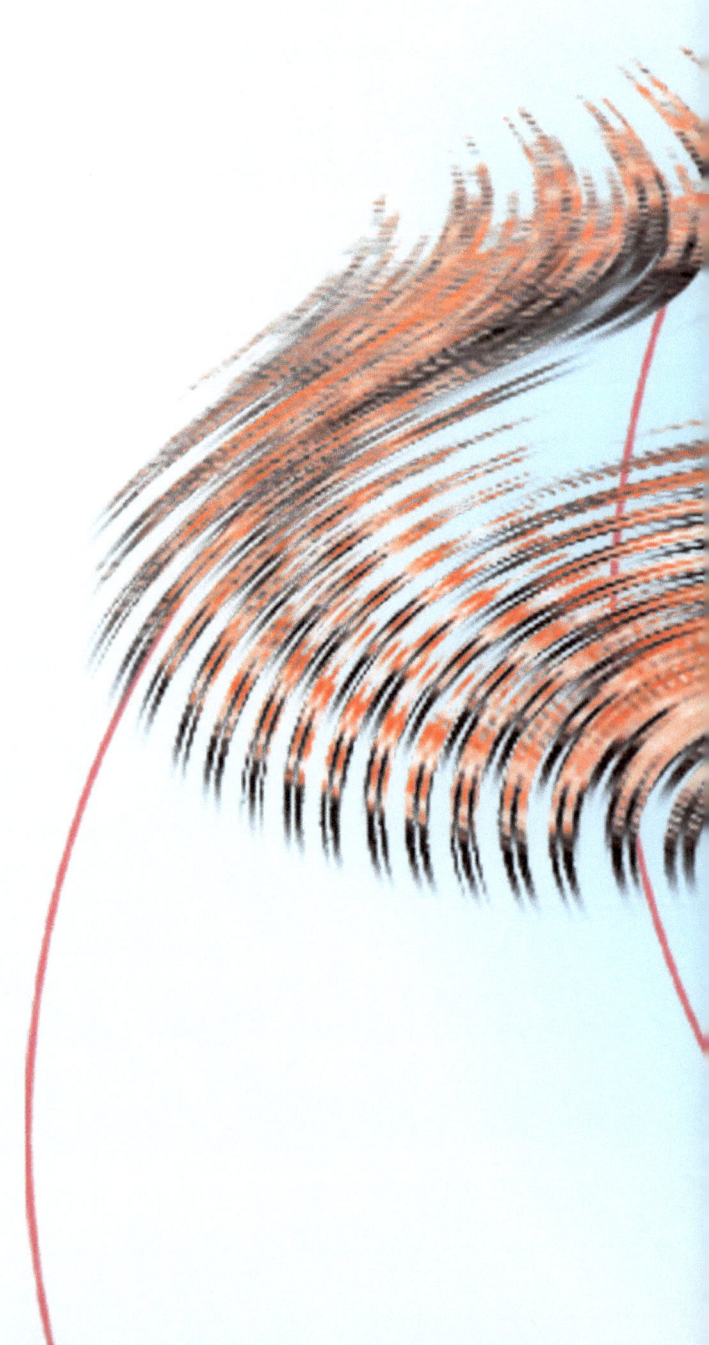

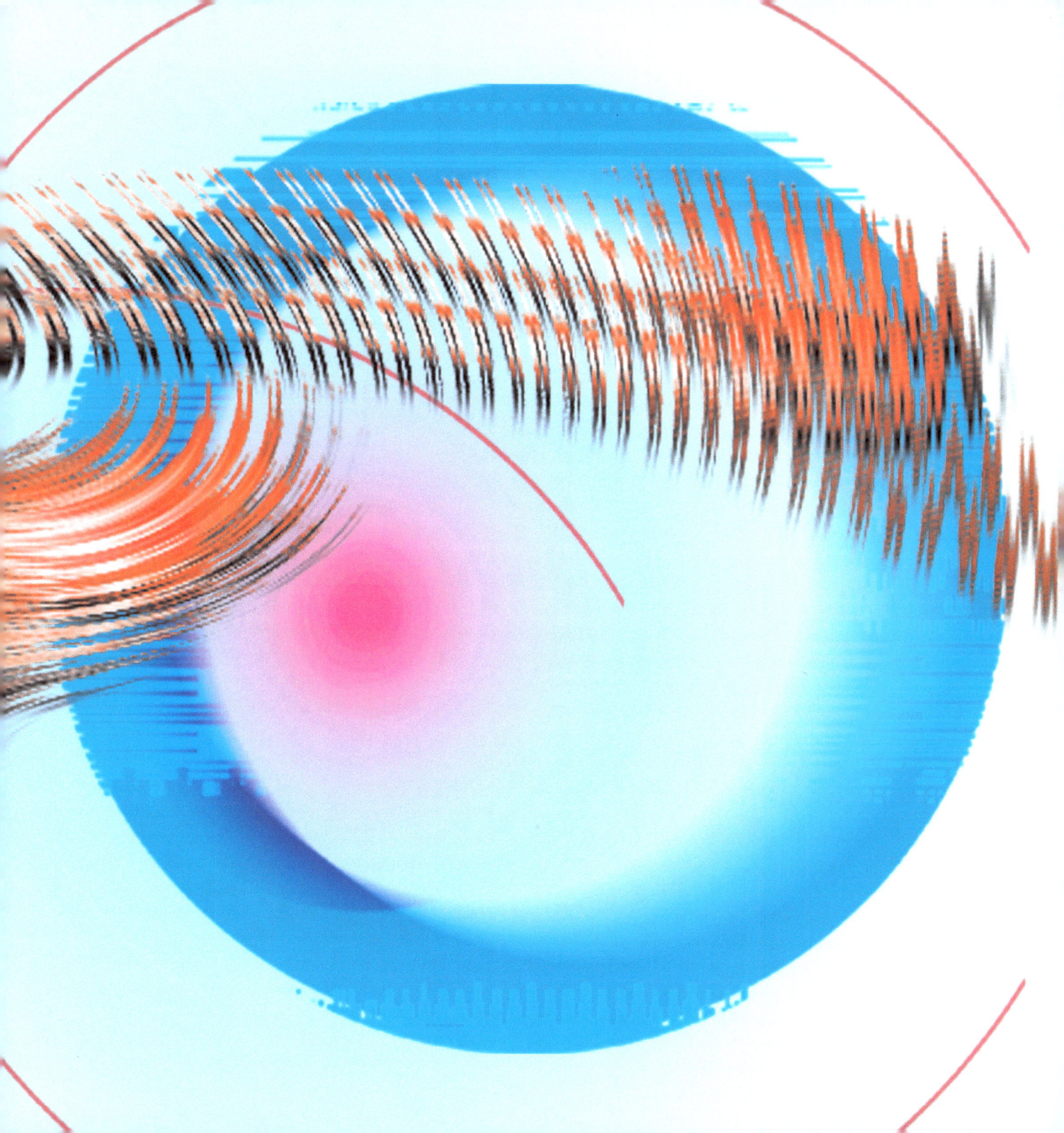

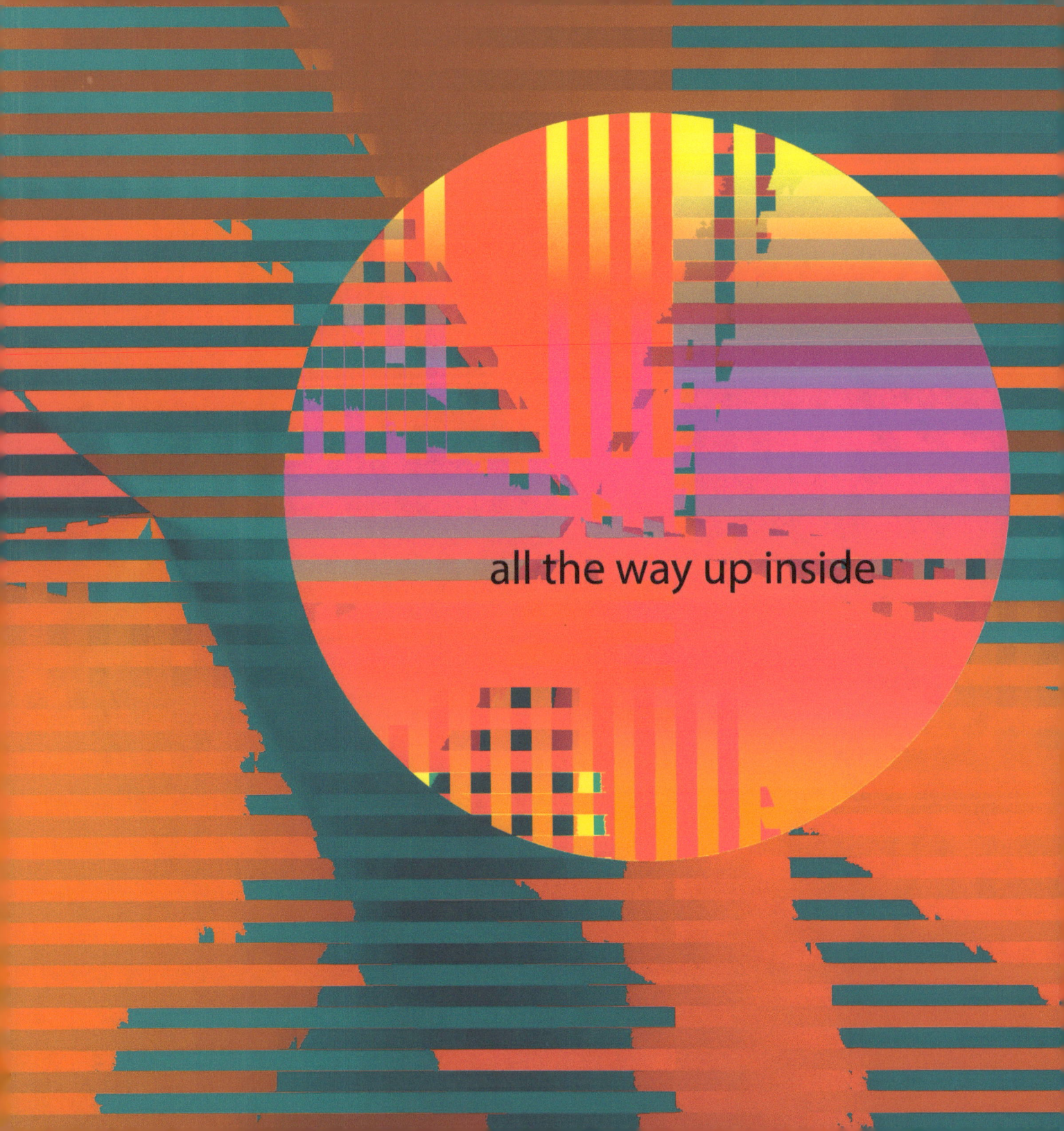

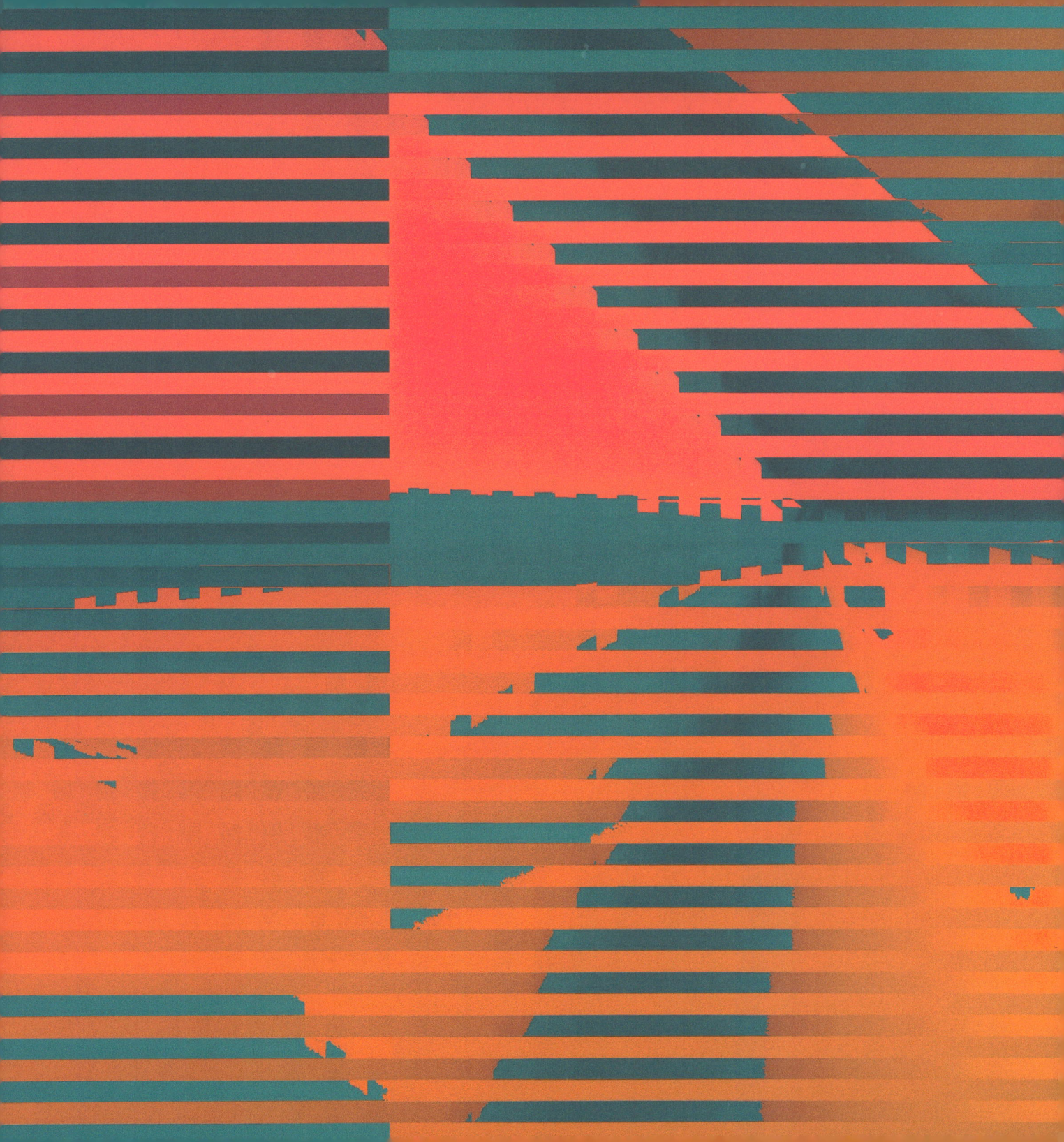

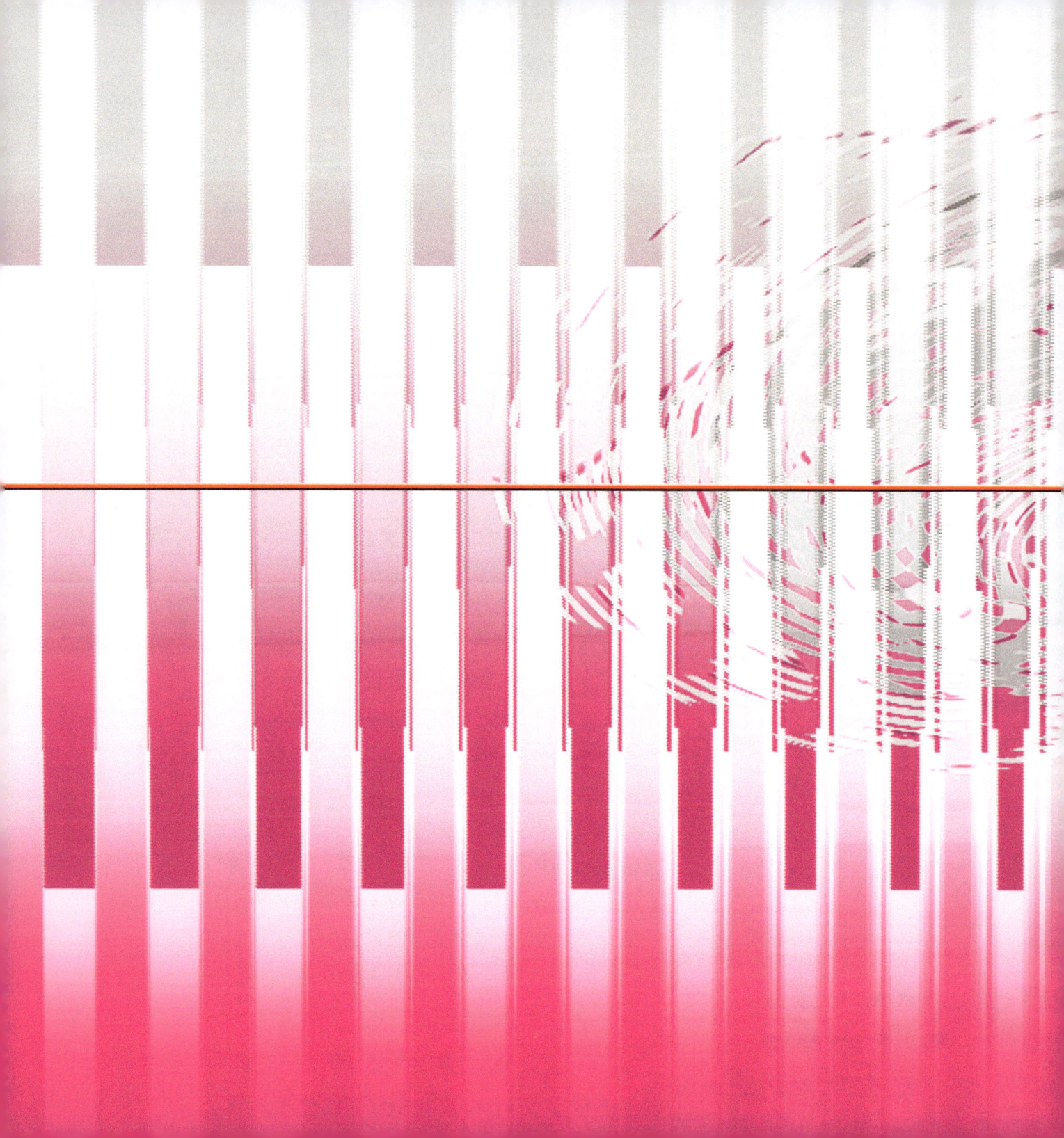

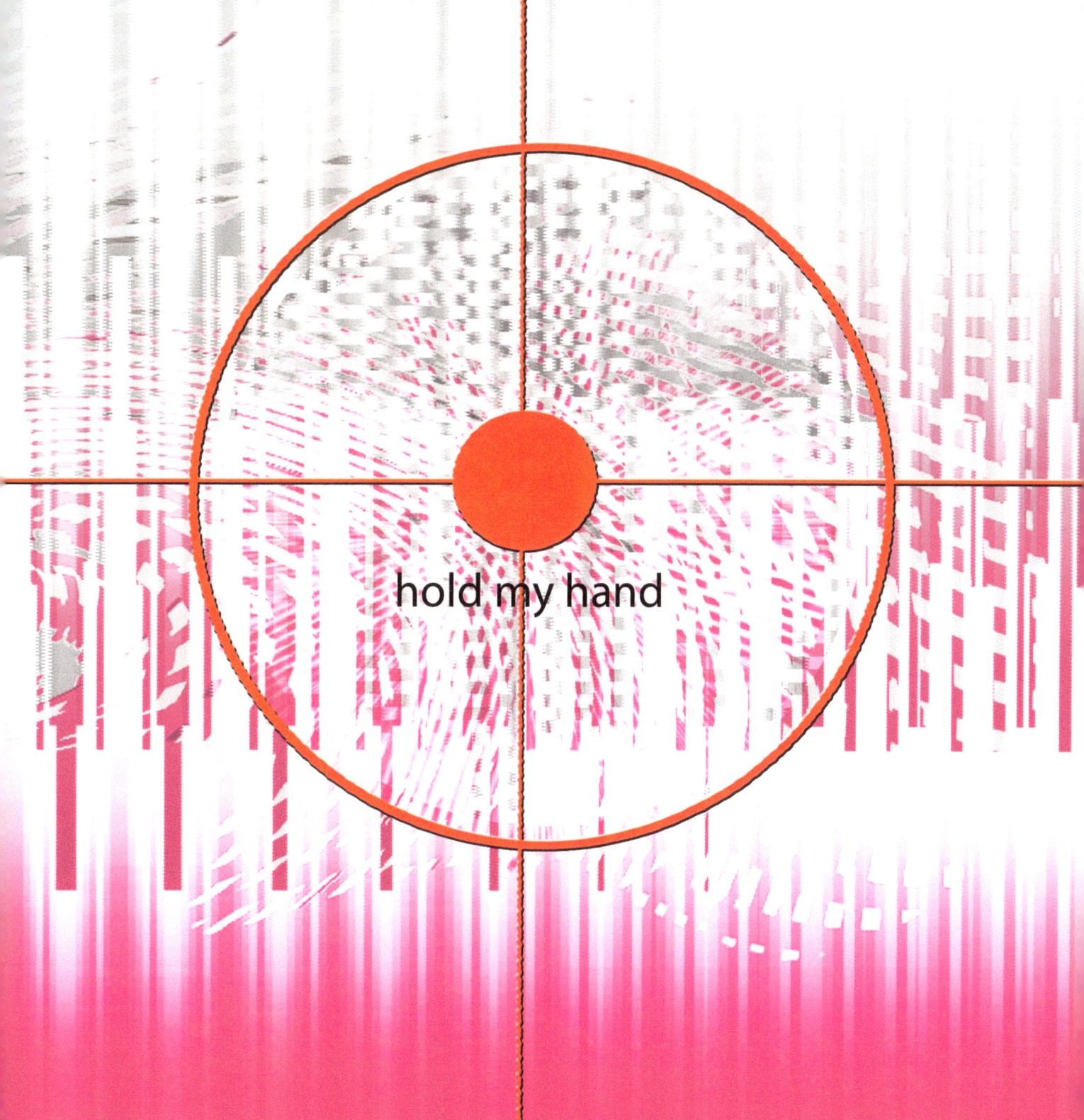

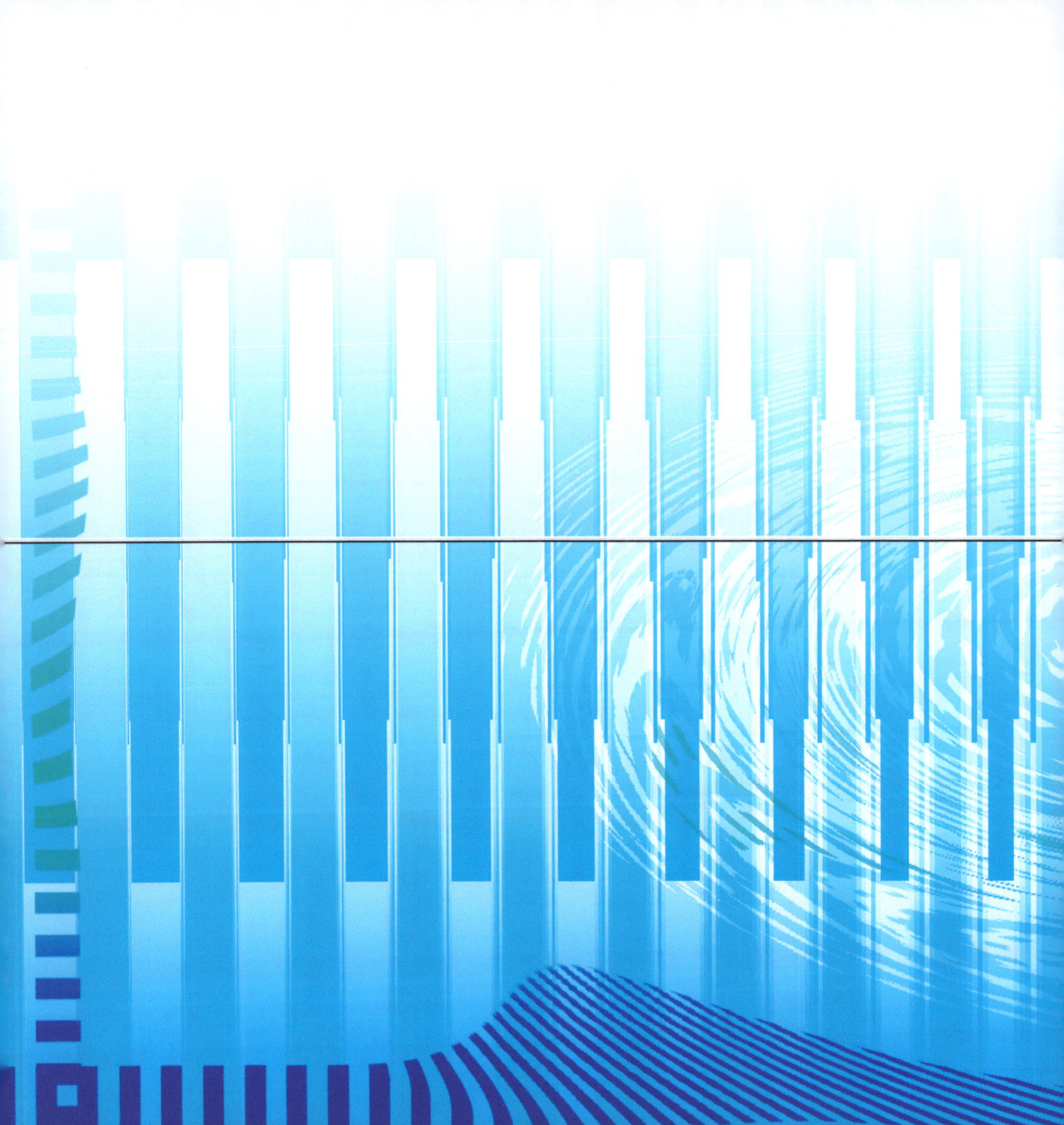

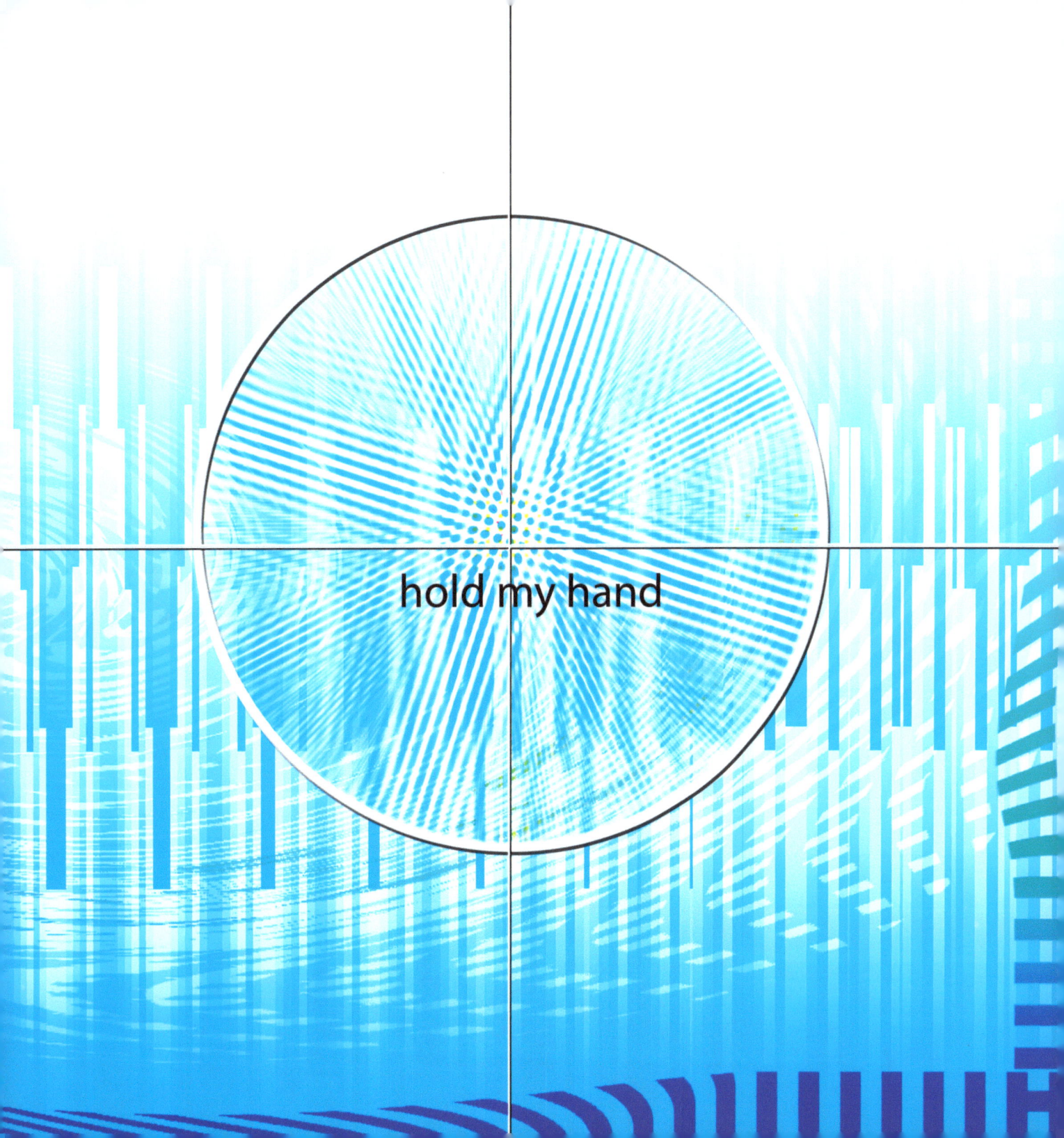

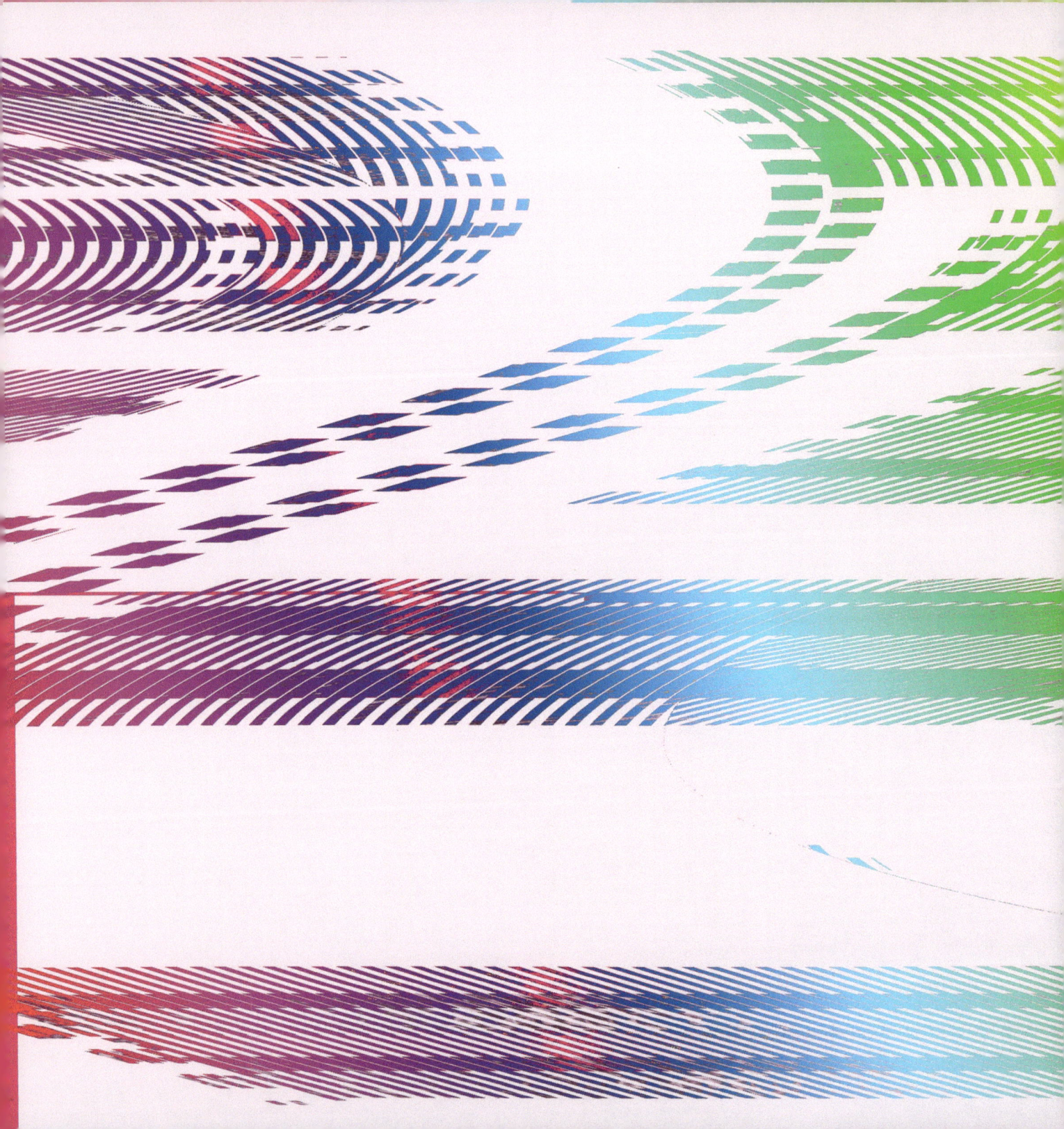

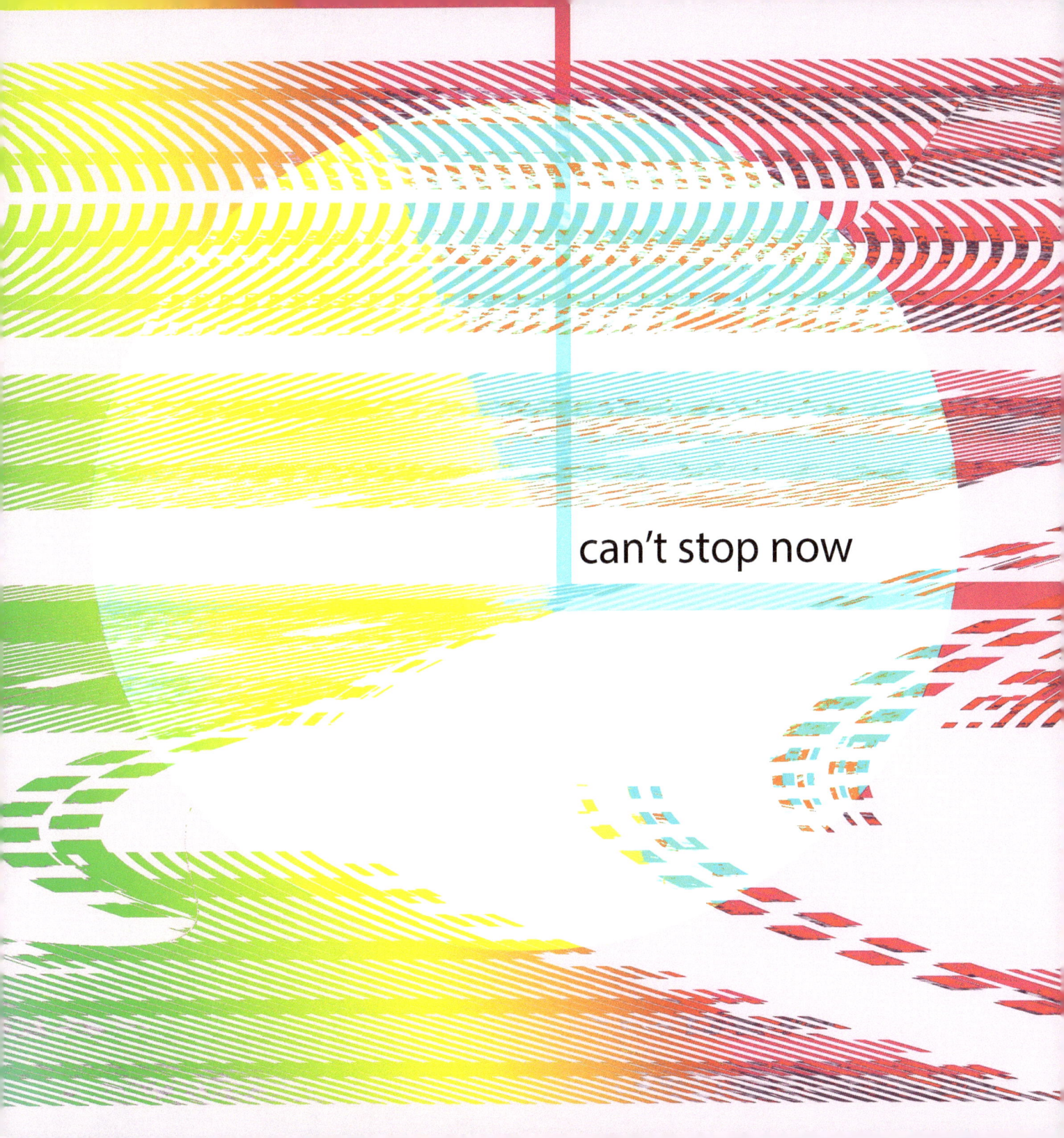

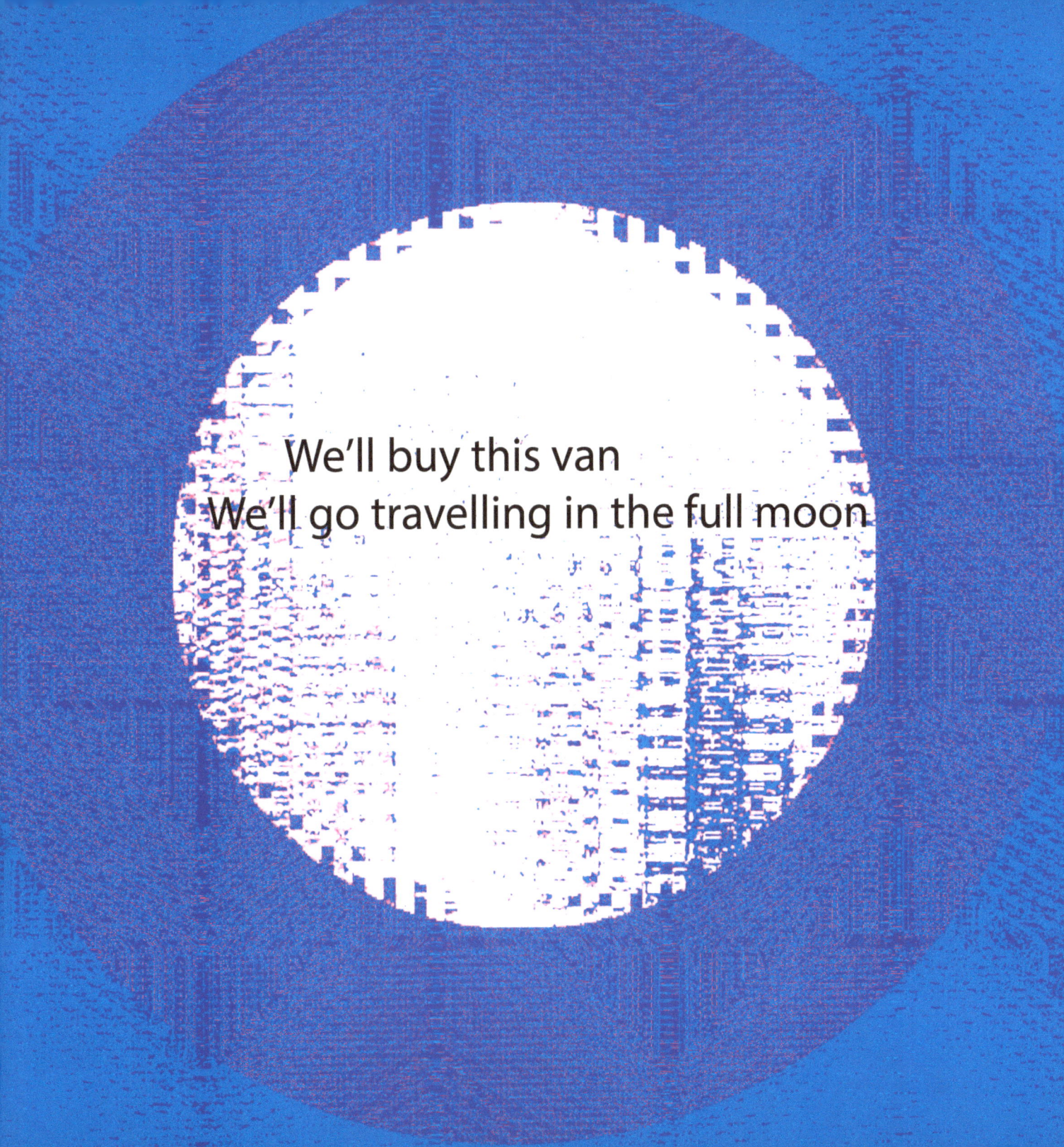

All Blown up

under the starlit sky

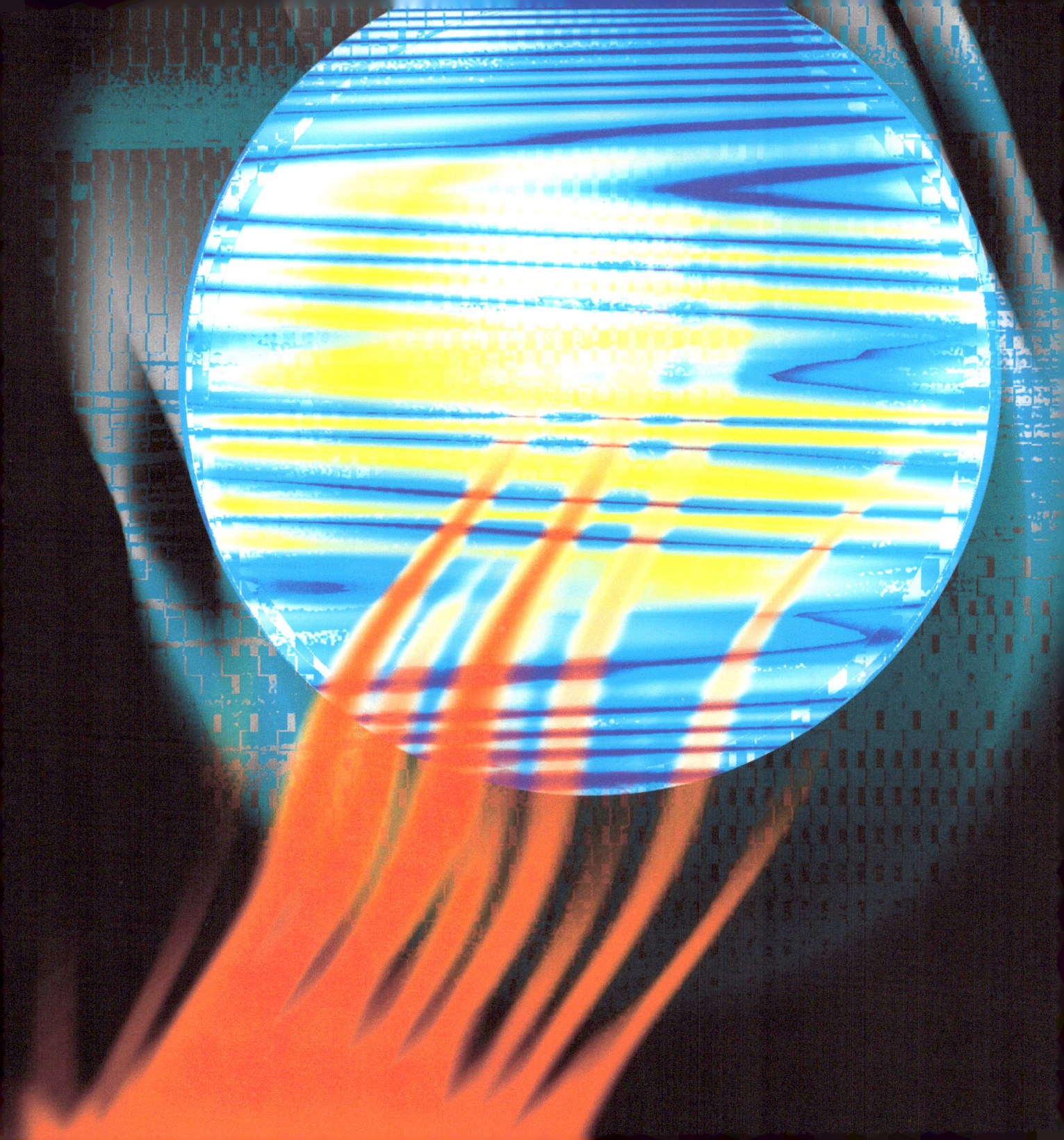

"Anyone searching for colourful, profound writing with a cavalcade of wonderful visual imagery would be overjoyed after reading Alexandra's books. They are truly wonderful.
The Grecian Poetess has managed to create a wonderful collection of wordage focusing on both the positive and negative aspects of life while leaving a glorious "taste" in the reader's mouth and eyes with the bright verbiage and great hypnotic usage of mesmerizing artistic counterparts. Find a beautiful shade fulfilling tree to perch under, read this wonderful book and the Muse of your soul will arise from her realm with a broad smile! And above all, you'll feel as if you know Ms. Psaropoulou!"

Joseph Cempa, Writer, 2016

"Myths and fairy tales violate determinism and they thus generate poetry. I think that this is what you do in your marvelous books. Poetry transcends reality. The fascination of quantum mechanics is precisely that it violates determinism of classical physics and generates something beyond ordinary reality."

Lambis Makrides, Physics Professor, 2015

www.ingramcontent.com/pod-product-compliance
Lightning Source LLC
Chambersburg PA
CBHW051209220526
45473CB00003B/958